BHAVISHYA MALIKA (ENGLISH)

PROPHECIES OF KALI YUGA AND KALKI AVATAR

SACHIN MOHAPATRA

Chennai • Bangalore

CLEVER FOX PUBLISHING
Chennai, India

Published by CLEVER FOX PUBLISHING 2025
Copyright © Sachin Mohapatra 2025

All Rights Reserved.
Paperback ISBN: 978-93-67074-31-2
Hardback ISBN: 978-93-67074-18-3

This book has been published with all reasonable efforts taken to make the material error-free after the consent of the author. No part of this book shall be used, reproduced in any manner whatsoever without written permission from the author, except in the case of brief quotations embodied in critical articles and reviews.

Content Disclaimer

This book is based on historical manuscripts, personal research, and interpretations. The author does not claim absolute authority over the predictions or prophecies mentioned. The *Bhavishya Malika* is an ancient collection of prophecies, and its meanings may vary based on interpretation. This work is presented solely for educational and informational purposes.

Liability Disclaimer

The author and publisher assume no responsibility for any actions taken based on the information provided in this book. The contents do not constitute professional, legal, medical, or spiritual advice.

Readers are solely responsible for how they interpret and apply the information. Any rituals, spiritual practices, or lifestyle choices inspired by this book should be approached with personal discretion and proper guidance.

Fair Use & Attribution Disclaimer

All referenced texts, quotes, and scriptures remain the intellectual property of their respective owners. They are used for educational and research purposes under fair use guidelines.

This book does not claim ownership over historical manuscripts or religious texts referenced within. If you believe any content infringes on copyright, please contact the publisher for resolution.

CONTENTS

About the Author .... *vii*
About the Book .... *xi*

Chapter 1. The Authenticity of Bhavishya Malika - Verified Manuscripts and Historical Evidence 1

Chapter 2. Mysteries of Kali Yuga - A Journey Into the Ancient Prophecies of Bhavishya Malika 6

Chapter 3. Lord of the Universe Mahaprabhu Jagannath 12

Chapter 4. The Five Divine Saints 18

Chapter 5. The Mystical Prophet of Kali Yuga - Saint Achyutananda Das 22

Chapter 6. Rise of Kalki - The Final Avatar of Lord Vishnu 28

Chapter 7. Secrets of Panchasakha and Bhavishya Malika 34

Chapter 8. Amarakosa Gita - Unraveling the Secrets of An Ancient Prophetic Manuscript 38

Chapter 9. Indra Govinda Gita - The Divine Prophecies of Jagannath Das 44

Chapter 10. The Lost Prophecies of Bhavishyata Parardha / Dibi Dibi Chautisha 49

Contents

Chapter 11.	Sunya Sanhita - The Mystical Prophecies of Mahapurusa Achyutananda Das	55
Chapter 12.	Chumbaka Malika - The Divine Secrets of Kali Yuga	61
Chapter 13.	Shiva Kalpa - The Prophecies of Saint Achyutananda Das	67
Chapter 14.	Jaiphula Malika - The Prophecies of Mahapurusa Achyutananda	73
Chapter 15.	Kaala Nirghanta - The Timelines of Destiny	79
Chapter 16.	The Hidden Meaning of Numbers, Years & Codes	84
Chapter 17.	Prophecies That Came True	88
Chapter 18.	The Beginning of World War 3 and Kali Yuga Mahabharata	94
Chapter 19.	The Final Leela of Lord Jagannath	101
Chapter 20.	Meena Shani - The Final Celestial Omen of Kali Yuga	106
Chapter 21.	Satya Yuga - Dawn of A New Age	110
Chapter 22.	The Final Revelation - Awakening to Truth	116

A Message From the Heart *120*

ABOUT THE AUTHOR

*F*ew dedicate their lives to uncovering ancient secrets, but for over a decade, I have been on a relentless mission to decode the lost prophecies of *Bhavishya Malika*—the most enigmatic manuscript of *Kali Yuga*. My name is Sachin Mohapatra, a native of Odisha, Bharat, a former mariner turned researcher, author, and digital influencer. What began as a childhood curiosity has now transformed into a divine calling to unveil the hidden truths of the universe.

From a young age, I was deeply influenced by the teachings of Maharshi Ved Vyas, Nostradamus, Saint Bhima Bhoi, and Baba Vanga. Their prophetic insights ignited a lifelong fascination with ancient wisdom and inspired my quest to decode the cryptic revelations of *Bhavishya Malika*.

The Bhavishya Malika, a monumental collection of over 100,000 palm leaf manuscripts authored by the revered *Panchasakha* of Odisha, holds the secrets of Kali Yuga, the rise of Kalki Avatar, and the final transformation of this world. These ancient texts not only prophesy global upheavals, wars, and spiritual awakenings but also explore cosmic mysteries, *tantra, mantra, yantra,* and the supreme force of *Parambrahma*. Remarkably, they were composed in a secret coded script—deliberately encrypted to protect this divine wisdom from misuse.

About the Author

For the past thirteen years, I have meticulously researched, analyzed, and decoded these sacred texts—often piecing together fragmented histories that few even know exist. My pursuit has not been easy; uncovering the hidden messages of time itself has required immense dedication, sacrifice, and an unwavering belief in the path of *Dharma*.

One pivotal moment in my journey came in 2011 when I deciphered a prophecy that foretold a devastating global crisis—one that mirrored the COVID-19 pandemic that shook the world in 2020. When the pandemic struck, I watched in awe and disbelief as the prophecy unfolded exactly as I had read years earlier. In that moment, I knew this knowledge could no longer remain hidden. The world needed to see, to understand, and to prepare. Just as Nostradamus' chilling forecasts have guided humanity through turbulent times, the revelations of Bhavishya Malika carry urgent messages for our future.

I became the first person to decode *Bhavishya Malika* and publish my research in Hindi on YouTube. Since then, my YouTube channel, Viral Odisha, has inspired over one lakh seekers, spreading positivity and spiritual awareness across Bharat and beyond. This book is not just a compilation of texts; it is a sacred offering—a tribute to *Mahaprabhu Jagannath* and a gift to those who have supported this cause with unwavering devotion.

As we stand on the brink of *Kali Yuga's* final years, my mission is to awaken humanity—to guide those who seek truth and to prepare for the great shift that lies ahead. Through this book, readers will not only gain insight into the future but will also find the wisdom needed to create a better, peaceful, and prosperous tomorrow.

Bhavishya Malika has remained hidden for centuries—until now. This is your chance to uncover its secrets and prepare for the transformation ahead. The final question remains: Are you ready?

ABOUT THE BOOK

Odia Verse:

"ଅଚ୍ୟୁତ କହନ୍ତି ବେଳ ହୋଇଗଲା ଆସି । ଭକତମାନଙ୍କୁ ଏବେ କହିବା ପ୍ରକାଶି ।"

- କାଳ ନିର୍ଘଣ୍ଟ, ଦ୍ୱିତୀୟ ସୁରସ

English Translation:

"Achyuta says, the time has come, let this wisdom enlighten all."

- *Achyutananda Das, Kala Nirghanta, 2nd Chapter*

In an age of confusion, deception, and relentless chaos, the world is desperate for truth. Hidden within the ancient manuscripts of Bhavishya Malika lies a wisdom so profound that it has remained concealed for centuries, waiting for the right moment to be unveiled. That moment is now.

For the first time in history, this book presents the world's first decoded, summarized, and translated edition of *Bhavishya Malika*, based on the original palm-leaf manuscripts written by the revered *Panchasakha* of Odisha. This is not merely a book—it is a gateway to a forgotten prophecy, a revelation that has been protected for generations, and a message meant for those who are destined to receive it.

About the Book

After more than thirteen years of relentless research, spiritual exploration, and decoding, I bring to light a tapestry of prophecies that have defied time itself—ancient revelations that foretell the fate of *Kali Yuga* and offer a glimpse into the age of Kalki Avatar. These manuscripts speak not only of the turbulence, wars, and spiritual decay of our times but also of the cosmic forces that govern existence, the mysteries of *tantra, mantra, yantra,* and the supreme consciousness of *Parambrahma*.

What makes these scriptures even more astonishing is that they were written in a secret coded script, deliberately encrypted to ensure that their sacred wisdom would not be misused in the darkest age of *Kali Yuga*. Now, after centuries of secrecy, these teachings have been revealed—not to a select few, but to all who seek the truth.

This book is not just an academic translation; it is a reconstruction of a lost legacy, a mission driven by an unshakable realization: that the truths hidden within *Bhavishya Malika* are more urgent now than ever before. Every prophecy decoded carries a message for this very era, guiding humanity through the chaos, deception, and destruction that threaten our world today.

In an age where misinformation reigns, *Bhavishya Malika Decoded* is a true compass for seekers—offering guidance, clarity, and the spiritual awakening that humanity desperately needs. This is not just a book to be read—it is a journey into the ancient future, where the wisdom of the *Panchasakha* illuminates the path forward.

The veil of secrecy has been lifted. The truth stands before you. This is your opportunity to understand the lost wisdom of *Bhavishya Malika* and its undeniable relevance in today's world.

Will you step into the light of ancient truth, or will you let history repeat itself?

CHAPTER 1

THE AUTHENTICITY OF BHAVISHYA MALIKA - VERIFIED MANUSCRIPTS AND HISTORICAL EVIDENCE

*B*havishya Malika has long captivated spiritual seekers and historians, yet its authenticity is sometimes questioned by skeptics. In this chapter, I address these doubts by providing verified evidence that several verified manuscripts of *Bhavishya Malika* are preserved in renowned institutions. My aim is to show that the prophecies and wisdom contained in these ancient texts are rooted in documented history and sustained through rigorous scholarly efforts.

Historical Background of the Manuscripts

The origins of *Bhavishya Malika* trace back to the 15th-16th century, when the texts were meticulously inscribed on palm leaves using traditional engraving methods. Over the centuries, these manuscripts have been carefully maintained despite numerous challenges, from natural decay and historical invasions. The esteemed *Panchasakha* entrusted many of these manuscripts to their disciples, who continued preserving them as a cherished family legacy.

Many of these texts remain hidden from the public to safeguard their divine knowledge. Some were even buried in secret locations across Odisha, to be unearthed only by selected individuals through specific divine mantras and *pujas,* upon receiving a telepathic divine order from Lord Jagannath. Additionally, numerous manuscripts are preserved in ancient temples and caves, where they are studied by sages and *rishi munis.*

Verified Sources and Manuscript Details

The authenticity of *Bhavishya Malika* is supported by original manuscripts housed in respected institutions. Below are the details of these sources:

1. Odisha State Museum, Bhubaneswar (India)

MANUSCRIPT NO.:	OL/1586
NAME OF MANUSCRIPT:	SUNYA SANHITA
AUTHOR:	ACHYUTANANDA DAS
MATERIAL:	PALM LEAF
LANGUAGE:	ODIA, SANSKRIT

2. Odisha State Museum, Bhubaneswar (India)

MANUSCRIPT NO.:	OL/1738
NAME OF MANUSCRIPT:	AMARA KOSHA GEETA
AUTHOR:	BALARAM DAS
MATERIAL:	PALM LEAF
LANGUAGE:	ODIA, SANSKRIT

3. Odisha State Museum, Bhubaneswar (India)

MANUSCRIPT NO.:	OL/647
NAME OF MANUSCRIPT:	BHAJANA TATWA
AUTHOR:	ANANTA DAS
MATERIAL:	PALM LEAF
LANGUAGE:	ODIA, SANSKRIT

4. Heidelberg University Library (Germany)

MANUSCRIPT NO.:	265 MSS 16/833
NAME OF MANUSCRIPT:	BHAVISHYA MALIKA
AUTHOR:	ACHYUTANANDA DAS
MATERIAL:	TRANSCRIBED
LANGUAGE:	ODIA, SANSKRIT

5. Heidelberg University Library (Germany)

MANUSCRIPT NO.:	265 MSS 16/220
NAME OF MANUSCRIPT:	AGATA BHAVISHYA LEKHANA
AUTHOR:	ACHYUTANANDA DAS
MATERIAL:	TRANSCRIBED
LANGUAGE:	ODIA, SANSKRIT

6. Heidelberg University Library (Germany)

MANUSCRIPT NO.:	265 MSS 16/182
NAME OF MANUSCRIPT:	GUPTA GITA
AUTHOR:	BALARAM DAS
MATERIAL:	TRANSCRIBED
LANGUAGE:	ODIA, SANSKRIT

Importance of These Manuscripts

The preservation of these manuscripts not only confirms the historical existence of *Bhavishya Malika* but also reinforces its credibility. Despite the passage of time and the challenges of preservation, these original texts have survived as tangible links to ancient wisdom. Their presence in globally recognized institutions underscores their scholarly and spiritual value. Moreover, the manuscripts provide compelling evidence that the prophecies recorded centuries ago continue to resonate with contemporary events, highlighting the enduring spiritual significance of the text.

Conclusion

These verified manuscripts preserved in the Odisha State Museum and the Heidelberg University Library serve as undeniable proof of *Bhavishya Malika's* authenticity. These records bridge the gap between ancient prophetic wisdom and modern scholarly research, offering a firm foundation on which to trust the text's spiritual and historical value. Beyond these verified sources, countless original palm leaf manuscripts remain safeguarded in secret chambers, temples, and caves across Odisha. These hidden archives invite readers to explore and independently verify the profound legacy of *Bhavishya Malika* as a guiding light through the complexities of Kali Yuga.

Disclaimer

This chapter presents information derived from verified historical records, authentic manuscripts, and traditional beliefs associated with *Bhavishya Malika*. References to divine messages, telepathy, and spiritual practices are drawn from ancient texts and are intended for educational and cultural understanding. Readers are encouraged to approach these insights with an open mind, respecting the spiritual significance these manuscripts hold in the cultural heritage of Odisha, India.

CHAPTER 2

MYSTERIES OF KALI YUGA - A JOURNEY INTO THE ANCIENT PROPHECIES OF BHAVISHYA MALIKA

Odia Verse:

"ନାହିଁ ବେଶିଦିନ ହେଲାଣି ନିକଟ କଳିଯିବ ଅପସରି ।
ସର୍ବେ ଏକମୁଖେ ଡାକିବେ ଜୟ ରାମକୃଷ୍ଣ ହରି ।"
- ଶିବକଳ୍ପ, ପଞ୍ଚଦଶ ନିର୍ଘଣ୍ଟ

English Translation:

"Not much time left, Kali Yuga's end is near.
All will chant—Jai Rama Krishna Hari for sure!"
  - Achyutananda Das, Shiva Kalpa, 5th Chapter

We are living in the final phase of Kali Yuga, the darkest and most deceptive era in human history. Ancient scriptures forewarned of this time—an age ruled by the demon Kali, where truth is buried under illusion, Dharma is mocked, and humanity is enslaved by greed, ignorance, and corruption. Unlike previous Yugas, where divine order prevailed, Kali Yuga is a battleground of deception, where the righteous struggle to survive while falsehood thrives as the new truth.

But this era of darkness is not eternal.

The *Bhavishya Malika,* inscribed on sacred palm leaf manuscripts by the revered *Panchasakha* of Odisha, unveils the final prophecy—a revelation that has remained hidden for centuries, now decoded and revealed for the modern world. The hour of reckoning is upon us.

The Eternal Yuga Cycle – The Wheel of Time

Time is not linear—it moves in divine cycles, known as *Satya Yuga, Treta Yuga, Dwapara Yuga,* and *Kali Yuga,* each repeating in an endless cosmic rhythm. Every Yuga marks a rise and fall of human consciousness. As Kali Yuga nears its final moments, the cycle prepares to reset, ushering in a new golden age of *Satya Yuga.*

The True Age of Kali Yuga – A Different Interpretation

While traditional Hindu texts claim that Kali Yuga lasts for 4,32,000 years, the *Bhavishya Malika* presents an alternate truth—the current duration is only 5,000 years. The rapid decline of Kali Yuga has been accelerated by humanity's collective sins, including:

- **Slaughtering of cows**
- **Destruction of unborn life**

- Atrocities against women and children
- Indulgence in unlawful and unnatural behaviors
- Disrespect toward deities and the degradation of Dharma
- Exploitation and abuse of nature's resources

These acts have pushed humanity to the brink, and the prophecies warn that we now stand at the edge of the final reckoning.

The Five Phases of Kali Yuga

According to *Bhavishya Malika,* Kali Yuga is divided into five distinct phases, each darker than the last:

1. *Treta Kali* (Already passed)
2. *Dwapara Kali* (Already passed)
3. *Ghor Kali* (Already passed)
4. *Ananta Kali* (Current Phase – The Final Darkness)
5. *Satya Kali* (The Dawn of the New Age)

We have already surpassed the darkest periods—and now stand at the final threshold of transformation.

The Yuga Sandhi Kaal – Era of Transition

The *Bhavishya Malika* speaks of *Yuga Sandhi Kaal,* a 200-year transitional phase between the end of Kali Yuga and the rise of Satya Yuga. This transition is divided into:

- *100 years of Sandhya Kaal* (**Dusk**) – This period has already concluded.

- *100 years of Pratah Kaal* (**Dawn**) – We are currently living through this final transition.

According to the ancient calculations, nearly 5,126 years have elapsed since the beginning of Kali Yuga. This means that we are now in its last stage—the final battle between darkness and light.

Ananta Kali & Satya Kali

- *Ananta Kali* – A time of divine intervention and purification.
- *Satya Kali* – The re-establishment of truth, law, and divine order.

The end of Kali Yuga will not be a silent transition—it will be a period of great turmoil, destruction, and renewal.

Who Will Rule the New Age?

In every Yuga, Lord Vishnu descends to restore Dharma, accompanied by Lord Ananta (Sesha Nag):

- *Treta Yuga* – Lord Ananta appeared as Sri Lakshman.
- *Dwapara Yuga* – He incarnated as Sri Balaram.
- *Kali Yuga* – He is prophesied to return as Sri Baladev or Balabhadra.

While many believe Lord Kalki will usher in *Satya Yuga*, the *Bhavishya Malika* reveals a deeper truth: Lord Ananta *(Balabhadra)* will rule the new era, restoring balance, justice, and divine order on Earth.

The End of Kali Yuga – A Prophetic Warning

The *Bhavishya Malika* foretells that Kali Yuga will end in fire, war, and devastation, marked by:

- **World War III** – A global war that will reshape the Earth.
- **Climate Catastrophes** – Natural disasters and environmental collapse.

Only a small fraction of humanity—those devoted to *Karma, Dharma*, and righteousness—will survive and lead the world into *Satya Yuga*.

The Choice of Humanity

We are no longer in the heart of Kali Yuga, but at its final, most critical moment. The *Bhavishya Malika* warns us:

A choice must be made:

- **Deception or Truth**
- **Darkness or Light**
- **Destruction or Salvation**

This is the last call—the final opportunity to awaken before the great transition begins.

The *Bhavishya Malika* is not just an ancient prophecy—it is a divine compass guiding seekers toward the new world. Those who wish to awaken must act now, for *Satya Yuga* is on the horizon.

The sands of time are running out. Will you awaken to the truth, or will you be lost in the final storm of Kali Yuga?

References:

The insights presented in this chapter are drawn from revered ancient texts, including:

- ***Brahma Vaivarta Purana*** – Narrated by Sri Krishna
- ***Shiva Kalpa & Naba Khanda Nirghanta*** – By Saint Achyutananda Das
- ***Kaala Nirghanta*** – By Saint Achyutananda Das
- ***Mahagupta Padmakalpa*** – By Panchasakha & Saint Arakhita Das

Disclaimer:

This interpretation is based on the ancient prophecies of *Bhavishya Malika* and personal research. Readers are encouraged to approach this content with an open mind and consider its spiritual and symbolic significance.

CHAPTER 3

LORD OF THE UNIVERSE MAHAPRABHU JAGANNATH

Odia Verse:

"ଶ୍ରୀ ପୁରୁଷୋତମ ଯାହାକୁ କହି । କ୍ଷେତ୍ର ମାନଙ୍କରେ କ୍ଷେତ୍ର ଅଟଇ । ଶ୍ରୀଦାରୁବ୍ରହ୍ମ ବିଜେ ଛନ୍ତି ଯହିଁ । ତାହାଙ୍କ ରାଜା ସୂର୍ଯ୍ୟବଂଶୀ ହୋଇ । ସେ ରାଜବଂଶ ଗୋଟି ଲୁପ୍ତ ହେବ । ସେ ଗାଦିରୁ ରାଜା ବୀଜ ବୁଡ଼ିବ ।"

— ଭବିଷ୍ୟତ ପରାର୍ଦ୍ଧ, ପ୍ରଥମ ପରାର୍ଦ୍ଧ

English Translation:

"The kingdom known as Purusottama stands as the greatest of all sacred lands. For Parambrahma Jagannath resides there, ruled by a king of the sun dynasty's heir. Yet this royal line will face its fall, with no successor to reign at all."

- *Achyutananda Das, Bhavishyata Parardha, 1st Parardha*

In the sacred expanse of *Akhand Bharat*, four divine *Dhams* are associated with the four great *Yugas*:

- **Badrinath Dham** – Established in Satya Yuga
- **Rameshwaram Dham** – Revered in Treta Yuga
- **Dwarka Dham** – Flourished in *Dwapara* Yuga
- **Puri Jagannath Dham** – The holiest site of Kali Yuga

Among these, Puri Jagannath Dham holds a unique and unparalleled significance, serving as the eternal seat of *Mahaprabhu Jagannath* in this age of darkness.

The Divine Significance of Puri Dham

The sacred land of Puri, Odisha, is often referred to as *Martya Vaikuntha*—the Earthly Abode of Lord Vishnu. Unlike other temples where deities are worshipped as idols, *Mahaprabhu Jagannath* is revered in his living form by millions of devotees.

- **Lord Hanuman**, as *Bedi Hanuman*, stands as the eternal guardian of this holy land.
- **Lord Shiva**, in his five-fold manifestation as *Pancha Mahadeva*, safeguards the temple's outer perimeter.
- **Goddess Mahamaya**, as *Bedha Kali*, protects the temple's inner sanctum.

Every element of Puri resonates with divine energy, making it a profound spiritual powerhouse in *Kali Yuga*.

Who is Mahaprabhu Jagannath?

Mahaprabhu Jagannath transcends all definitions, embodying the essence of universal divinity:

- To some, he is Krishna; to others, Rama.
- *Shaktas* see him as Goddess Kali; *Ganapatyas* recognize his presence in Ganesha.
- *Buddhists* perceive him as Buddha; followers of other faiths see him as the embodiment of supreme consciousness.

The name Jagannath is derived from three Sanskrit words:
- **Ja** (ज) – Birth
- **Gan** (ग) – Creation or Movement
- **Nath** (नाथ) – Lord or Controller

Thus, Jagannath means "The Lord Who Governs the Universe." In this dark age of *Kali Yuga*, he has descended to protect his devotees from the grip of evil.

Parambrahma: Supreme Soul of the Universe

In the grand cosmic design, everything—planets, stars, gods, even Brahma, Vishnu, and Mahesh—has a finite existence. They appear, play their divine roles, and eventually merge back into the eternal force.

But one truth remains eternal—Parambrahma, the Supreme Soul of the Universe.

- *Parambrahma* is beyond time and space. Unlike all celestial beings, he has no beginning, no end.
- He is the source of all creation, yet remains beyond form—neither male nor female, neither physical nor ethereal.
- He exists as an infinite, radiant energy, beyond human perception, rotating like a luminous white sphere of cosmic power.

The ancient seers meditated upon this formless *Parambrahma* and discovered the Tribeej Tatva—the Three Seeds of Creation:
- **Brahma** – The Creator
- **Vishnu** – The Preserver
- **Maheshwara** – The Destroyer

From this cosmic trinity, the entire universe was formed—from galaxies and stars to every living being on Earth.

The *Bhavishya Malika* describes that in *Kali Yuga*, *Parambrahma* descends to Earth in his purest form, and that form is none other than *Mahaprabhu Jagannath*.

Jagannath Tatva: The Mystery of the Divine Form

Mahaprabhu Jagannath is not an idol; he is the physical embodiment of Parambrahma. His mysterious appearance carries profound meaning:

- **No legs** – Symbolizing omnipresence, moving without physical movement.
- **No hands** – Representing omnipotence, acting without direct action.
- **No eyelids** – Signifying omniscience, observing the universe unceasingly.

His divine form is not bound by human perception. When devotees stand before *Jagannath's chaturbhuja* form, they experience an inexplicable energy, a vibration that resonates through their body and soul.

The Secret of the Wooden Deity

Unlike conventional idols, *Lord Jagannath's* deity is sculpted from sacred neem wood, chosen through a mystical process. This divine form contains a hidden essence known as Brahma *Padartha*—a cosmic element representing *Parambrahma* himself.

This is why, during *Rath Yatra*, when millions witness his chariot procession, even the air seems charged with divine energy.

Kalki Avatar: The Final Incarnation of Lord Vishnu

According to *Bhavishya Malika*, the final avatar of Lord Vishnu—*Kalki*—will be unlike any previous incarnation. He will not just be an aspect of Lord Vishnu; he will be Mahaprabhu Jagannath himself, appearing in human form.

- He will arrive at the peak of Kali Yuga's destruction.
- He will annihilate the forces of darkness and restore Dharma.
- His divine rule will mark the transition into Satya Yuga.

Just as Sri Rama came in *Treta Yuga* and Sri Krishna in *Dwapara Yuga*, *Bhavishya Malika* proclaims that in this age, *Mahaprabhu Jagannath* will descend as Sri Kalki, bringing an end to darkness.

Conclusion: The Divine Sovereign of the Universe

Mahaprabhu Jagannath is not just a deity—he is the living presence of Parambrahma. He is the eternal force that governs the cosmos, the guardian of Dharma in Kali Yuga, and the divine protector of all beings.

His eternal presence in *Puri Dham* serves as divine assurance that in the darkest age of *Kali Yuga*, his devotees will always find refuge in his grace.

Those who seek truth and righteousness will witness the rise of a divine kingdom on Earth, led by the eternal power of *Mahaprabhu Jagannath*.

References:

The insights and information presented in this section are drawn from revered ancient texts and spiritual manuscripts, including:

- ***Skanda Purana*** – Attributed to Maharishi Ved Vyas
- ***Niladri Mahodaya*** – Narrated by Lord Brahma
- ***Guru Bhakti Gita*** – Authored by Saint Achyutananda Das
- ***Sunya Sanhita*** – Authored by Saint Achyutananda Das
- ***Anadi Sanhita*** – Authored by Saint Achyutananda Das

CHAPTER 4

THE FIVE DIVINE SAINTS

Odia Verse:

"ଆଗମ ଭାବ ଜାଣେ ଯଶୋବନ୍ତ । ଗାରକଟା ଯନ୍ତ୍ର ଜାଣେ ଅନନ୍ତ । ଆଗତ ଅନାଗତ ଅଚ୍ୟୁତ ଭଣେ । ବଳରାମ ଦାସ ତତ୍ତ୍ୱ ବଖାଣେ । ଭକ୍ତିର ଭାବ ଜାଣେ ଜଗନ୍ନାଥ । ପଞ୍ଚସଖା ଏ ଉତ୍କଳ ମହନ୍ତ ।"

English Translation:

"Jasobanta deciphers the scriptures profound, Ananta masters the yantra's sound. Achyuta foresees both future and past, Balaram reveals the tatva that will last. Jagannath embodies devotion's flame, These five Saints — divine in name."

In the rich spiritual heritage of Odisha, the Panchasakha hold an unparalleled place. The word *Pancha* means "five," and *Sakha* means "friends." These five great Saints and poets—Achyutananda Das, Ananta Das, Jasobanta Das, Jagannath Das, and Balaram Das—were not only ardent devotees of Mahaprabhu Jagannath but also profound visionaries, mystics, and literary scholars. Their divine mission was not just to spread devotion but to foresee the destiny of humanity and guide seekers through the darkness of

Kali Yuga. Each of these revered Saints played a crucial role in shaping Odia spiritual literature, guiding seekers, and preserving divine wisdom for future generations. Below is a brief account of their lives, contributions, and legacies.

Achyutananda Das: The Prophet of the Future

Among the Panchasakha, Achyutananda Das is widely regarded as the greatest mystic and seer. He is best known for his prophetic writings, compiled in a monumental work known as Malika, which contains detailed predictions about the future of the world, humanity, and *Kali Yuga*.

- **Birthplace**: Tilakana, Nemala, Cuttack, Odisha

Achyutananda Das was not only a poet but also a spiritual scientist who studied human Physiology, Ayurveda, and Astrology. His works emphasize the unity of all religions and the imminent arrival of the divine Kalki Avatar.

Sisu Ananta Das: The Spiritual Poet

Sisu Ananta Das was a key figure in Odia spiritual literature, particularly during the Bhakti movement. His teachings bridged the gap between *Jnana Yoga* (the path of knowledge) and *Bhakti Yoga* (the path of devotion), making his work deeply influential.

- **Birthplace:** Balipatana, Khordha, Odisha

    His visionary poetry and devotion continue to guide seekers toward self-realization and divine consciousness.

Jasobanta Das: The Mystic Philosopher

Jasobanta Das was a mystic, philosopher, and profound scholar. His deep knowledge of scriptures allowed him to explore esoteric wisdom, consciousness, and the eternal truths of the universe.

- **Birthplace:** Adhanga, Jagatsinghpur, Odisha

His teachings emphasize the union of the individual soul with the Supreme Consciousness and the importance of inner awakening.

Jagannath Das: The Great Litterateur

Jagannath Das, honored with the title Atibadi (meaning "very great"), was an eminent Odia poet and scholar. His greatest contribution was translating the *Bhagavata Purana* into Odia, making sacred knowledge accessible to the common people.

- **Birthplace:** Puri, Odisha

His devotional writings remain widely read, shaping the spiritual culture of Odisha.

Balaram Das: The Eldest and Wisest

The eldest among the Panchasakha, Balaram Das was a poet, philosopher, and devoted follower of Lord Jagannath. His *Lakshmi Purana* challenged social discrimination and promoted gender equality and universal devotion.

- **Birthplace**: Puri, Odisha

His teachings emphasize compassion, morality, and divine justice, making him a revolutionary spiritual leader of his time.

The Eternal Legacy of the Panchasakha

The Panchasakha were not just poets or Saints—they were spiritual revolutionaries, divine messengers, and bearers of ancient wisdom. They carried the light of Mahaprabhu Jagannath into the world, their words echoing across centuries.

Their prophecies, devotion, and literary contributions form the spiritual foundation of Odisha and continue to shape the hearts of millions who seek the path of truth, devotion, and ultimate liberation.

Their words are not relics of the past—they are living prophecies, waiting to be understood.

Those who seek truth will find their path illuminated by the wisdom of the Panchasakha, for their teachings are eternal, transcending time and space.

References:

The insights and information presented in this section are drawn from revered ancient texts and spiritual manuscripts, including:

- *Brahma Sankuli* – Authored by Saint Achyutananda Das
- *Anakara Sanhita* – Authored by Saint Achyutananda Das
- *Chhayalisa Patala* – Authored by Saint Achyutananda Das

Disclaimer on Historical Dates:

The birth and death dates of the Panchasakha remain uncertain due to the lack of definitive historical documentation.

CHAPTER 5

THE MYSTICAL PROPHET OF KALI YUGA - SAINT ACHYUTANANDA DAS

Odia Verse:

"ନଳୀନ ବନ ଲୁଚିଛି ନେମାଳ ଗ୍ରାମରେ । ଲୀଳା ଯେ ପ୍ରକାଶ ହେବ ଆଦ୍ୟ ସେହିଠାରେ । ନାଶ ଯିବେ ଦୁଷ୍ଟ ଲୋକ ହେବ ହାଣ ଗୋଳ । ଲୀଳା ଦେଖୁଥିବ ବସି ଅଚ୍ୟୁତ ପାମର ।"
   - ଅଚ୍ୟୁତାନନ୍ଦ ଦାସ, କଳିଯୁଗ ମାଳିକା, ପ୍ରଥମ ଅଧ୍ୟାୟ

English Translation:

"Hidden lies the Nalina grove in Nemala's sacred land, Where the divine play will unfold as fate has planned. Wicked ones shall perish, chaos will rage, Achyuta, the humble, will witness this age."
   - Achyutananda Das, Kaliyuga Malika, 1st Chapter

Few Saints in history have bridged the gap between prophecy and reality like Saint Achyutananda Das. A mystic, poet, and visionary, his words echo across centuries, guiding humanity through the storm of Kali Yuga. Revered as a fountainhead of spiritual wisdom, mysticism, and devotional literature, his life was a divine mission—to awaken mankind and preserve sacred knowledge for future generations.

- **Birthplace and Family:**

Mahapurusa Achyutananda was born in Tilakana village, Cuttack district, Odisha. His parents, Dinabandhu Khuntia and Padmavati Devi, were devout Vaishnavites. According to legend, his birth was foretold by Mahaprabhu Jagannath.

- **Divine Conception:**

Odia traditions hold that, Padmavati Devi had a vision of Lord Jagannath, who blessed her with a divine child. Mahapurusa Achyutananda is considered an *Ayonija* (born without natural conception), signifying his supernatural origin.

- **Birth Name:**

Originally named Achyuta, one of the epithets of Lord Vishnu, he embodied divine wisdom from birth

- **Education and Early Studies:**

From childhood, Mahapurusa Achyutananda displayed extraordinary intellect. Under the guidance of great spiritual masters, including Chaitanya Mahaprabhu, he mastered the *Vedas, Puranas, Upanishads,* and occult sciences.

Previous Births

According to the Bhavishya Malika, Mahaprabhu Jagannath revealed that Saint Achyutananda Das has incarnated in all four ages, each time serving Lord Vishnu:

- In **Satya Yuga,** he was Rishi Krupajala.
- In **Treta Yuga,** he was Nala.
- In **Dwapara Yuga,** he was Sudama.
- In **Kali Yuga,** he is Achyuta.

Future Births

Mahapurusha Achyutananda prophesied that he would take a total of 13 births in Kali Yuga. His 12th birth was as Saint Hadi Das of Chhatia Dham, while his 13th birth has already occurred, awaiting the unfolding of his final *Leela*.

Spiritual Journey and Role as a Poet

1. The Panchasakha Connection:

Mahapurusa Achyutananda was one of the legendary *Panchasakha* (Five Friends)—divine scholars and visionaries who revolutionized Odia literature and devotion to Mahaprabhu Jagannath.

2. Contributions to Odia Literature:

His works include over a million verses, primarily in *Achyutananda Malika*, covering prophecy, devotion, and cosmic mysteries:

- **Bhavishya Malika** – Prophetic texts foretelling the future of Kali Yuga.
- **Gopalanka Gita** – Devotional songs dedicated to Sri Krishna.
- **Haribansha** – A narrative on the divine pastimes of Lord Krishna.
- **Sunya Sanhita** – A metaphysical discourse on the concept of the void (*Sunya*).

3. Bhakti and Social Reform:

Beyond his role as a saint, Mahapurusa Achyutananda was a social reformer. He challenged religious hypocrisy, opposed caste discrimination, and emphasized devotion (Bhakti) as the true path to liberation.

Bhavishya Malika – Prophecies of Kali Yuga

The *Bhavishya Malika,* attributed to Saint Achyutananda, contains cryptic predictions about the modern world:

- **Environmental Changes** – Predictions of climate anomalies and natural disasters.
- **Societal Decay** – Forewarnings about moral collapse, corruption, and war.
- **Arrival of Kalki Avatar** – the prophesied descent of Vishnu's final incarnation.

Many of these prophecies are encoded and decipherable only by the spiritually awakened.

Mysticism and Yogic Powers

1. Siddhis and Divine Healing:

Mahapurusa Achyutananda was renowned for miraculous healing abilities and spiritual powers, many of which have been documented in folklore and temple records.

2. Kundalini Awakening:

He wrote extensively on the seven chakras, Kundalini energy, and meditation techniques, revealing ancient spiritual secrets.

3. Concept of Sunya – The Void:

Mahapurusa Achyutananda emphasized the *Sunya Purusha* (Formless Supreme Being)—an infinite energy beyond human comprehension.

Samadhi and Eternal Legacy

1. Samadhi at Nemala:

Mahapurusa Achyutananda consciously left his physical body in Nemala, Odisha, where his *samadhi* shrine remains a revered spiritual site.

2. Teachings on Death and Liberation:

He taught that death is only a transition and that detachment, devotion, and Dharma lead to Moksha (liberation).

3. Cultural and Spiritual Impact:

Mahapurusa Achyutananda's palm-leaf manuscripts are preserved in secret monasteries, govt. museums and secret temples, continuing to guide seekers and scholars alike.

Unique Facts About Saint Achyutananda Das

- **Multilingual Scholar** – Wrote in Odia, Sanskrit, and hybrid languages.
- **Preserved in Palm-Leaf Manuscripts** – His teachings were transcribed on palm leaf by his disciple Ram Das.
- **Deeply Connected to Jagannath Culture** – His teachings emphasize Mahaprabhu Jagannath as Parambrahma (Supreme Soul Of The Universe).

Final Thoughts: A Messenger of Destiny

Mahapurusa Achyutananda Das was not just a Saint—he was a prophet, a visionary, and a divine messenger. His words were not mere poetry; they were codes of cosmic truth, revealing the past, present, and future.

Even today, as the world plunges deeper into Kali Yuga, his words echo from sacred palm-leaf manuscripts, whispering timeless wisdom to those willing to listen.

The question remains—will you awaken to his message before time runs out?

References:

The insights and information presented in this section are drawn from revered ancient texts and spiritual manuscripts, including:

- *Brahma Sankuli* – Authored by Saint Achyutananda Das
- *Anakara Sanhita* – Authored by Saint Achyutananda Das
- *Chhayalisa Patala* – Authored by Saint Achyutananda Das
- *Kaliyuga Malika* – Authored by Saint Achyutananda Das

Disclaimer:

The information presented here is based on traditional beliefs, historical manuscripts, and widely accepted spiritual interpretations. While every effort has been made to ensure accuracy, certain historical details may vary across sources. Readers are encouraged to approach this work with an open mind, considering its cultural and spiritual significance.

CHAPTER 6

RISE OF KALKI - THE FINAL AVATAR OF LORD VISHNU

Odia Verse:

"ଗୁପ୍ତ ଗ୍ରନ୍ଥ ଅଛି ନେମାଳ ବଟରେ ସେବେଳେ ହେବ ବାହାର ।
କଳଙ୍କୀ ମନ୍ତ୍ର ଯେ ପ୍ରକାଶଟି ହେବ ସତ୍ୟ ସତ୍ୟ ଏହି ଗାର ।"
- ଅଚ୍ୟୁତାନନ୍ଦ ଦାସ, ଚକଡ଼ା ମଡ଼ାଣ, ଅଚ୍ୟୁତ ଉବାଚ

English Translation:

"A secret scripture lies beneath nemala's sacred banyan tree; it shall emerge when the time must be. Kalki mantra will shine bright and far, this is the truth, the sacred scar."
- Achyutananda Das, Chakadamadana, Words Of Achyuta

The most fierce and powerful incarnation of Lord Vishnu is the Kalki Avatar. According to the ancient prophecies of the *Bhavishya Malika*, Lord Kalki will be born to Sri Vishnuyasa, a devout follower of Lord Vishnu, and Mata Padmavati, a devoted worshipper of Maa Lakshmi. His birthplace is prophesied to be the divine land of Sambhala or Sambhal Nagar, believed by certain interpretations to be situated between Cuttack and Jajpur Districts in the state of Odisha.

The Mysterious Birth of Kalki

Odia Verse:

"ଆକାଶରେ ଯେଉଁଦିନ ଦେବ ଧ୍ୱଜା ପଡ଼ି ଥିବଟି ଜାଣ ଲୋ ଜାଇଫୁଲ । ସେହିଦିନ ପ୍ରଭୁ ହେବେ ଜନ୍ମ ।"
- ଅଚ୍ୟୁତାନନ୍ଦ ଦାସ, ଜାଇଫୁଲ ମାଳିକା, ଅଚ୍ୟୁତ ଉବାଚ

English Translation:

"The day a falling star with a blazing tail appears in the sky, mark my words — Lord Kalki will be born on that very day."
- Achyutananda Das, Jaiphula Malika, Words Of Achyuta

Prophecies from the revered Panchasakha suggest that Lord Kalki has already descended to Earth, with his birth believed to have taken place between 1990 – 1991. However, by divine design, his identity remains concealed from the public until the destined time.

In today's world, false prophets and self-proclaimed Saints often misuse this prophecy, claiming to be Kalki. Such deceitful claims aim to manipulate faith for personal gain. True devotees understand that an avatar of Lord Vishnu reveals himself through actions, not empty proclamations.

The authentic presence of Lord Kalki will be known not through fame or propaganda but by his deeds. His role is destined to be recognized through the immense impact of his actions on humanity and the restoration of dharma (righteousness).

Kalki's Hidden Years

According to the *Bhavishya Malika*, Lord Kalki will remain concealed until humanity reaches the peak of its moral and spiritual decline. The darkness of Kali Yuga will intensify before his emergence, as corruption, violence, and ignorance dominate the world.

His silence is not inactivity but preparation. During this period of concealment:

- He will acquire celestial weapons and divine knowledge, preparing for his cosmic mission.
- The universe will align to signal the nearing end of Kali Yuga.
- Only the spiritually awakened will begin to sense the shifting energies heralding his arrival.

When the moment is right, he will rise with unimaginable power, destined to confront the forces of adharma (unrighteousness) and lead humanity into a new era.

The Signs of Kalki's Arrival

The *Bhavishya Malika* provides cryptic signs of his emergence:

- **Cosmic Disturbances:** Unusual planetary alignments and celestial phenomena will mark his coming.
- **Global Upheaval:** Widespread wars, natural disasters, and societal collapse will precede his appearance.

- **Rise of Falsehood:** As deception reigns supreme, those devoted to truth and dharma will begin to recognize subtle signs of Kalki's presence.

His return will not be announced with grand declarations but will be felt in the hearts of true devotees and sages across the world.

Kalki's Divine Purpose

When the world stands on the brink of collapse, Lord Kalki will rise as the harbinger of Satya Yuga—the age of truth and righteousness. Mounted on his celestial white horse, Devadatta, and wielding his divine sword, he will lead the charge against darkness and restore balance to the universe.

His divine mission includes:

- **Annihilating Evil:** Destroying those who spread adharma and corruption.
- **Restoring Dharma:** Re-establishing universal laws of truth, justice, and morality.
- **Rebuilding Civilization:** Laying the foundation for a new era of enlightenment and spiritual awakening.

This will not be an ordinary battle—it will be a cosmic cleansing, ending the chaos of Kali Yuga and ushering in a golden age.

The Call for Devotees: Preparing for Kalki's Arrival

As humanity teeters on the edge of destruction, the responsibility falls on true seekers and devotees to remain steadfast in their faith. Only those who uphold truth, practice compassion, and live by dharma will recognize the signs of Kalki's emergence.

The choice before humanity is clear:

- Embrace **righteousness** or fall into **ignorance**.
- Walk the path of **truth** or succumb to **deception**.
- Choose **spiritual awakening** or face **destruction**.

The rise of Lord Kalki is not just a prophecy—it is a cosmic certainty, a divine promise that darkness will be vanquished and a new era of peace, justice, and enlightenment will begin.

References:

The insights and information presented in this section are drawn from revered ancient texts and spiritual manuscripts, including but not restricted to:

- *Amara Jumara Sanhita* – Authored By Saint Achyutananda Das
- *Hadi Das Malika* – Authored By Saint Hadi Das (12th birth of Saint Achyutananda Das)
- *Shiva Kalpa O Naba Khanda Nirghanta* – Authored by Saint Achyutananda Das
- *Agata Bhavishya* – Authored By Saint Jagannath Das
- *Jaiphula Malika* – Authored By Saint Achyutananda Das

Disclaimer

Some facts and details mentioned in the *Bhavishya Malika* have been intentionally omitted from this work due to their confidential and sacred nature. This decision has been made out of deep respect for the sanctity of this divine knowledge and to avoid any potential misinterpretations. The essence of this work remains dedicated to truth, spiritual awakening, and the service of dharma.

CHAPTER 7

SECRETS OF PANCHASAKHA AND BHAVISHYA MALIKA

Odia Verse:

"ଗୁରୁ ପାଦଧାୟୀ ନେମାଳ ବଟରୁ କହୁଛି ଗୁପତଜ୍ଞାନ ।
ମୁର୍ଖେ କହିବୁ ନାହିଁ ସପ୍ତ ବାର ରାଣ ଦେଲି ତହିଁ ।"
— ଅଚ୍ୟୁତାନନ୍ଦ ଦାସ, ଚକଡ଼ା ମଡ଼ାଣ, ପ୍ରଥମ ଅଧ୍ୟାୟ

English Translation:

"At my Guru's feet, I humbly confide, revealing the hidden truth kept inside. Speak not to fools; let wisdom reside, Swear it to me seven times with pride."
— Achyutananda Das, Chakadamadana, 1st Chapter

The Panchasakha—Achyutananda Das, Jagannath Das, Ananta Das, Balaram Das, and Jasobanta Das—were not merely poets or Saints. They were visionaries, seers, and divine messengers entrusted with profound spiritual revelations. Their mission was clear: to preserve Sanatana Dharma in the dark age of Kali Yuga and prepare mankind for the arrival of Kalki Avatar.

Unlike other Saints who focused solely on bhakti (devotion), the Panchasakha delved into occult sciences, tantric wisdom, and esoteric prophecies. They foresaw that Kali Yuga would be an era of deception and turmoil, so they encrypted their knowledge in symbolic language—ensuring that only the worthy and enlightened could decipher it.

Their most secretive knowledge is the Malika or Bhavishya Malika, a collection of divine prophecies containing precise revelations about global wars, social upheavals, natural disasters, and the ultimate restoration of dharma. Many of these predictions have already come true, while others remain locked in mystery, awaiting their destined unveiling.

The Hidden Nature of Bhavishya Malika

The Bhavishya Malika is not a single text but a vast collection of prophetic scriptures. Many of these writings remain concealed, awaiting their destined discovery. Ancient accounts state that many of these palm-leaf manuscripts still remain buried under temples, submerged in riverbeds, sealed within ancient caves and safeguarded by secret lineages of monks.

These texts are not ordinary writings—they contain layers of hidden meanings, numerical codes, and esoteric references. The unenlightened see only riddles, but those with spiritual awakening can decode their true essence. Mahapurusa Achyutananda foresaw the corruption of knowledge in Kali Yuga and deliberately ensured that the most powerful prophecies would remain veiled until the right moment.

Even today, certain portions of the Malika are recited in secret yogic gatherings across Odisha.

Panchasakha's Trikala Drishti

The Panchasakha possessed Trikala Drishti, the divine ability to perceive past, present, and future. This extraordinary insight allowed them to foresee events centuries before their occurrence, such as:

- Cataclysmic natural disasters signaling the nearing end of Kali Yuga
- Global wars that will redefine world power structures
- The rise of false prophets who will mislead humanity
- The final battle between dharma and adharma, paving the way for Kalki Avatar

Many of these prophecies have already unfolded with chilling accuracy, while others remain hidden in time, waiting for their inevitable fulfillment.

The Eternal Mystery of the Panchasakha

Beyond their scriptures, the Panchasakha themselves remain an enigma. Ancient sources suggest they were not ordinary humans but divine beings reincarnated across different yugas. This implies that their mission extends beyond a single lifetime—a continuous divine intervention across ages to uphold dharma. Their teachings, encrypted in mystical texts, are meant for those destined to awaken and lead humanity through the final transformation.

Conclusion: The Awaited Revelation

The secrets of Panchasakha and Bhavishya Malika are not relics of the past; they are a living mystery that continues to unfold. These manuscripts, their hidden messages, and the ancient places preserving this divine knowledge all point to something far greater than mere historical texts.

As Mahapurusa Achyutananda foretold:

"When the darkest hour of Kali Yuga arrives, a chosen one will unveil the true meanings of Malika, and the lost scriptures will resurface to guide humanity."

For centuries, countless seekers have attempted to decipher these sacred manuscripts, yet their deepest truths remained elusive. Now, for the first time, their most guarded secrets are about to be unveiled—secrets that may alter the very destiny of Kali Yuga itself…

CHAPTER 8

AMARAKOSA GITA - UNRAVELING THE SECRETS OF AN ANCIENT PROPHETIC MANUSCRIPT

Odia Verse:

"ପିଣ୍ଡ ବ୍ରହ୍ମାଣ୍ଡର ବ୍ୟବସ୍ଥା । ଶୁଣ ଅର୍ଜୁନ ମହାଜ୍ଞାତା ।
ଯାହା ଦେଖୁଅଛୁ ଏହି ବ୍ରହ୍ମାଣ୍ଡେ । ସମସ୍ତ ଅଛଇ ଏହି ପିଣ୍ଡେ ।
ଏ ତତ୍ତ୍ୱ ଯେ ଜନ ଜାଣିବ । ଘୋର ସଂସାରୁ ତରିଯିବ ।"

- ଅମରକୋଷ ଗୀତା, ଦ୍ୱିତୀୟ ଅଧ୍ୟାୟ

English Translation:

"The body and the cosmos are one. Listen, O Arjuna, with wisdom divine. All that you perceive in this vast universe dwells within this very form. He who realizes this eternal truth shall break free from the endless cycle of worldly storms."

- Amarakosha Gita, 2nd Chapter

Odia Verse:

"ପାଷଣ୍ଡ ଠାରେ ନ ପଢ଼ିବୁ । ମୋ ପାଦପଦ୍ମ ଛୁଇଁଥିବୁ ।
ବ୍ରହ୍ମା ନ ପାରେ ଏହା ଜାଣି । ତୋତେ ମୁଁ କହିଲି ବଖାଣୀ ।
ଯେ ସାଧୁ ଆଣି ତା ପଢ଼ିବ । ଆମ୍ଭାର ଭାବ ସେ ଜାଣିବ ।"

— ଅମରକୋଷ ଗୀତା, ତୃତୀୟ ଅଧ୍ୟାୟ

English Translation:

"Do not let this sacred knowledge fall into the hands of the wicked; promise me by my lotus feet that you shall guard it. Even lord brahma himself cannot comprehend this wisdom, yet I am revealing it now to you. Only a true seeker who reads this with pure devotion shall grasp the essence of this divine revelation."

— *Amarakosha Gita, 3rd Chapter*

The Legacy of Saint Balaram Das

The Amarakosa Gita, authored by Saint Balaram Das—one of the legendary Panchasakha—serves as a spiritual beacon, illuminating profound insights into the cosmic order, human nature, and the divine cycle of existence. It is not just a manuscript but a celestial roadmap guiding humanity toward enlightenment amid the turmoil of Kali Yuga. This text is said to have been narrated by Lord Shiva to Goddess Parvati, drawing reference from the divine conversation between Lord Sri Krishna and Pandu Putra Arjuna in the *Mahabharata*.

Saint Balaram Das, one of the five revered Panchasakha of Odisha, was a visionary poet, mystic, and philosopher. His writings, deeply devoted to Lord Jagannath, are renowned for their emphasis on universal compassion, social equality, and the omnipresent divine essence within all beings. His spiritual genius transcended time, weaving together the esoteric knowledge of the *Vedas, Mahabharata,* and *Puranas* into accessible teachings for the common people.

The *Amarakosa Gita* is one of his most profound works, composed in ancient Odia, rich with metaphysical wisdom. It serves as a crucial part of the prophetic tradition of *Bhavishya Malika*, revealing timeless guidance for humanity's moral and spiritual evolution.

Essence of the Amarakosa Gita: Unveiling the Mystical Teachings

Instead of overwhelming the reader with complex interpretations, this chapter provides a structured overview of the core themes embedded in this manuscript:

- **The Ultimate Truth: Parambrahma Tatva and Brahmagyana**

The Amarakosa Gita explores the nature of Supreme Consciousness (Parambrahma Tatva) and the essence of divine knowledge (Brahmagyana), revealing how spiritual enlightenment liberates one from the cycle of birth and death.

- **The Primordial Sound: Omkara and Ekakshara Tatva**

The text describes the supreme power of the cosmic sound 'Om' and its connection to the eternal truth. The Ekakshara Tatva—the singular vibrational essence—holds the key to unlocking the mysteries of existence.

- **The Microcosm and Macrocosm: Pinda-Brahmanda Tatva**

"Pinda and Brahmanda are one and the same," proclaims the text, emphasizing that the human body *(Pinda)* is a miniature representation of the entire cosmos *(Brahmanda)*. Understanding this profound connection leads to liberation from the material illusion.

- **Creation and Illusion: The Divine Play of Maya**

The manuscript explores the origins of creation, the expansion of life forms, and the cosmic illusion *(Maya)* that binds beings to material existence. It warns of the deceptive nature of worldly pleasures and urges seekers to rise above illusion.

- **The Yogic Path and the Six Chakras**

The text elaborates on the intricate system of *Yoga*, detailing the importance of breath control, meditation, and the activation of the six *chakras* to attain spiritual elevation.

- **The Decline of Dharma in Kali Yuga**

The *Amarakosa Gita* predicts the moral and spiritual degradation in Kali Yuga, highlighting rampant corruption, social unrest, and the loss of righteousness. Yet, it reassures that divine intervention will restore balance.

- **Rebirth and the Return of Divine Beings**

The manuscript mentions the rebirth of the Pandavas in Kali Yuga, the divine presence of Lord Jagannath, Balabhadra, and

Subhadra, and their role in guiding humanity through the final phase of cosmic transformation.

- **The Elemental Force: The Significance of Vayu (Air) Tatva**

The text speaks of *Vayu* as the carrier of life force (Prana), vital for sustaining existence and spiritual elevation.

- **Why the Amarakosa Gita Still Resonates Today**

Despite being centuries old, the teachings of the *Amarakosa Gita* remain strikingly relevant in today's world. The manuscript offers profound reflections on morality, self-discipline, and spiritual awakening, providing a guide to navigating modern struggles.

- **A Timeless Guide for a Chaotic Era**

While deeply rooted in ancient wisdom, the *Amarakosa Gita* speaks directly to contemporary seekers. It encourages self-reflection, ethical living, and spiritual growth amidst material distractions. In a world dominated by uncertainty and moral ambiguity, this sacred text reminds us of the eternal power of *Dharma*.

Conclusion: The Eternal Light of Amarakosa Gita

The *Amarakosa Gita* is not just a manuscript—it is a divine revelation. Through the prophetic voice of Saint Balaram Das, it reminds us that even in the darkest times of Kali Yuga, the light of *Dharma* can guide humanity toward balance, enlightenment, and ultimate liberation. This sacred text continues to inspire, offering valuable lessons for those who seek clarity, truth, and spiritual awakening in a world poised for transformation.

By embracing the wisdom of the Amarakosa Gita, one does not merely read a text but embarks on a profound spiritual journey—a journey that leads to the realization of the eternal truth that governs all existence.

CHAPTER 9

INDRA GOVINDA GITA - THE DIVINE PROPHECIES OF JAGANNATH DAS

Odia Verse:

"କଳିଯୁଗରେ କଳଙ୍କି ଅବତାର । ଦୁଷ୍ଟ ନିବାରଣ ବାନା ତାହାର । ଏହା ବିଚାରି କହ ହୃଷୀକେଶ । କେ ଅବା ରହିବ କେ ଅବା ନାଶ ।"

— ଇନ୍ଦ୍ର ଗୋବିନ୍ଦ ଗୀତା, ପ୍ରଥମ ଅଧ୍ୟାୟ

English Translation:

"In Kali Yuga, Kalki Avatar is the banner of destruction for the wicked. Considering this, tell me, O Hrushikesh, who will remain and who shall perish?"

— Indra Govinda Gita, 1st Chapter

Odia Verse:

"ନାନା ବ୍ୟାଧ୍ୟ, ପୀଡା, ରୋଗ ଘଟିବ । ବୈଦ୍ୟ ବ୍ୟାଧୂକି ଔଷଧ ନ ଦେବ । ମୋର ବାକ୍ୟ ଅପ୍ରମାଣ କରିବେ । ଅର୍ଥ ଲୋଭରେ ସମସ୍ତେ ମାତିବ ।"

— ଇନ୍ଦ୍ର ଗୋବିନ୍ଦ ଗୀତା, ଶ୍ରୀକୃଷ୍ଣ ଉବାଚ

English Translation:

"Various diseases, suffering, and plagues shall arise. Even physicians will fail to provide a cure. People will dismiss my words as untrue. Everyone will be blinded by greed for sure."

— *Indra Govinda Gita*, Words of Lord Sri Krishna

The Celestial Revelation: A Dialogue Between Indra and Govinda

Deep within the esoteric prophecies of *Bhavishya Malika* lies the mystical Indra Govinda Gita—a divine conversation between Indra, the king of the celestial realms, and Govinda, the eternal Lord Krishna. Composed by the revered Saint Jagannath Das, this manuscript unravels the hidden truths of the cosmic order, the cyclical descent of divine incarnations, and the ominous fate of Kali Yuga.

Through this sacred dialogue, the Lord unveils the past, present, and future—guiding humanity through the darkness of ignorance and leading them toward the light of devotion. This timeless scripture foretells the cataclysms of Kali Yuga, the trials of Dharma, and the final advent of the supreme warrior—Kalki Avatar.

The Ten Avatars: The Eternal Cycle of Divine Descent

The *Indra Govinda Gita* begins by recounting the ten divine incarnations (Dashavatar) of Lord Vishnu, who appear in different ages to restore cosmic balance. Each avatar carries a unique mission—to protect Dharma, destroy evil, and uplift the righteous.

But the most crucial revelation in this scripture concerns the final avatar—Kalki. Unlike the earlier incarnations, Kalki comes not to establish peace but to cleanse the world with fire and sword. His divine play (*Leela*) will shake the very foundations of existence, and his celestial companions (*Sahacharis*) will assist him in the great war against the forces of darkness.

The Fate of Kali Yuga: Signs of the End Times

The *Indra Govinda Gita* describes the relentless decay of *Kali Yuga*, where morality fades, deception thrives, and spiritual wisdom is ridiculed. The scripture precisely predicts:

- The brutal Mughal invasion, the desecration of temples, and the attack of Kala Pahada on Odisha—events that changed the course of history.
- The great wars fought in the land of Bharata (India) before independence, highlighting the relentless struggles for righteousness.
- The destruction destined for Jagannath Puri in the end times—a powerful cyclone that will strike the sacred temple, symbolizing the influence of Kali over divine realms.

- The rise of pandemics, tsunamis, earthquakes, and economic collapse—unfolding as divine punishments for humanity's moral decay.

The Rise of the Pure Devotees: The Warriors of Dharma

Amidst this chaos, *Indra Govinda Gita* reveals the hidden warriors of Kali Yuga—the secret devotees who shall stand with Kalki during the final battle. Unlike ordinary mortals, these enlightened souls have walked unnoticed among men, preserving Dharma in silence. When the final hour arrives, they will rise, guided by divine command, to fulfill their cosmic purpose.

This prophecy echoes the ancient understanding that true devotion does not seek recognition—it thrives in solitude, awaiting the moment when righteousness must reclaim the world.

The Punishment of the Wicked and the Decline of Civilization

The scripture explicitly warns that those who embrace falsehood, greed, and treachery shall face divine judgment. Their wealth will turn to dust, their power will crumble, and they shall wander in darkness. The mighty rulers of the world, who once controlled entire nations, will beg for a drop of water in the final days of Kali Yuga.

The greatest punishment will not be physical suffering but spiritual abandonment—the ultimate curse where the divine presence withdraws, leaving the souls of sinners to wither in an abyss of their own making.

The Final Transition: The Dawn of Satya Yuga

The *Indra Govinda Gita* does not end in despair but in hope. After the great purification, when the storms have passed and the wicked have fallen, a new age will arise—*Satya Yuga*. The earth shall heal, Dharma will be restored, and the sacred names of Hari will once again echo across the land.

Only those who have upheld virtue, devotion, and humility shall witness this divine transition. Those who seek the truth must prepare—not through worldly means but through unwavering surrender to the Supreme.

Conclusion: The Urgency of Devotion

The *Indra Govinda Gita* is not merely a prophecy; it is a warning, a guide, and a divine revelation for those who wish to survive the storms of Kali Yuga. In this era of uncertainty, where chaos reigns and deception flourishes, the only salvation lies in devotion to the eternal truth.

The words of Jagannath Das serve as a beacon, reminding us that time is fleeting, and the cycle of *Yugas* is relentless. The age of Kalki is near—who will stand, and who will fall? The answer lies within our choices today.

Let us embrace the wisdom of this sacred text, surrender to the divine, and walk the path of Dharma before the final hour arrives.

CHAPTER 10

THE LOST PROPHECIES OF BHAVISHYATA PARARDHA / DIBI DIBI CHAUTISHA

Odia Verse:

"ସତ୍ୟ ସତ୍ୟ ଏହା ତ୍ରିବାର ସତ୍ୟ । ଏ ଗ୍ରନ୍ଥ ପଢ଼ିବ ମୋହରି ଭକ୍ତ । ମୂର୍ଖକୁ ଏ ଗ୍ରନ୍ଥ ବିଷ ଲାଗିବ । ପଢ଼ିଶୁଣି ଗଲେ ପାଶୋରି ଯିବ ।"

— ଭବିଷ୍ୟତ ପରାର୍ଦ୍ଧ, ପ୍ରଥମ ପରାର୍ଦ୍ଧ

English Translation:

"Mark my words, this manuscript will unfold, Only my devotee shall grasp what's told. For the ignorant, like poison it shall be, They'll read a bit, then let it be."

— Bhavishyata Parardha, 1st Parardha

Odia Verse:

"କଳିଯୁଗ ଶେଷ ହୋଇବା ବେଳେ । ଏହି ତିନିକଥା ହୋଇବ ତାଳେ । ରାଜାଜାତି ହାଡ଼ି ବେମାରୀ ବାଢ଼ି । ଜଗତେ ଫେରିବ ଲୁହାରକଢ଼ି । ପନ୍ଦର ସତର କର ବାନ୍ଧିବ । ମୀନ ଶନି ତହିଁ ଯୁକ୍ତରେ ଥିବ ।"

— ଭବିଷ୍ୟତ ପରାର୍ଦ୍ଧ, ଚତୁର୍ଥ ପରାର୍ଦ୍ଧ

English Translation:

"At the end of Kali Yuga, when Saturn aligns in Pisces' reign, Sickness will strike both the rich and the plain. Industries will rise and flourish once more, As burdensome taxes knock on every door."

— *Bhavishyata Parardha, 4th Chapter*

The Sacred Traditions of Odisha: A Glimpse into the Divine Manuscript

In the sacred traditions of Odisha, where time intertwines with eternity, there exists a rare and cryptic manuscript—*Bhavishyata Parardha*, also known as *Dibi Dibi Chautisha*. This divine scripture, narrated by the enlightened Saint Achyutananda Das and penned by Balaram Das in the presence of the revered Sisu Ananta Das, reveals a hidden dimension of time itself. It speaks not just of the past and present, but of an unfathomable future, etched in celestial decrees.

The Hidden Places of Odisha: Gateways to the Divine

Within the folds of this manuscript lie secrets of ancient places in Odisha, places unknown to the modern world yet holding immense spiritual power. These locations, veiled by time and karma, serve as cosmic nodes, where the energies of the divine directly interact with the terrestrial plane. The scriptures hint at hidden temples, underground chambers, and mystic caves where enlightened beings continue their *sadhana*, untouched by the corruption of Kali Yuga.

The Wars of the End Times: The Clash of Dharma and Adharma

As foretold, an era of great upheaval shall descend upon the world. The wars of the end times are inevitable—battles not just of kingdoms, but of righteousness versus deception, devotion versus delusion. This text vividly describes the coming of cataclysmic conflicts, where nations will rise and fall, and *dharma* shall be put to its ultimate test. The warriors of this war are not merely mortals but incarnations of past *yugas,* returning to fulfill their divine obligations.

The Rulers of Kali Yuga: Kings and Their Fate

Kali Yuga is the era where kings shall forsake *dharma*, and the throne shall be occupied by those driven by greed and arrogance. The manuscript outlines the cycles of rulers in this age, from the noble-hearted to the tyrannical, leading up to the prophesied arrival of Kalki—the final avatar of Lord Vishnu. It warns of deceitful leaders who will pose as protectors but will usher the world into chaos, only to be overthrown by divine will.

The Hidden Leelas of Kalki Avatar

Unlike popular portrayals, *Bhavishyata Parardha* sheds light on the lesser-known acts (leelas) of Kalki. Before his final revelation, he shall walk unnoticed, testing devotees, correcting dharma, and setting the stage for the world's renewal. It speaks of the divine army that shall rise alongside him—warriors concealed in ordinary forms, awaiting the call to restore righteousness.

Jagannath Dham: The Spiritual Anchor of Kali Yuga

No prophecy is complete without the mention of Puri Jagannath Dham, the heart of cosmic energy in Kali Yuga. This text emphasizes its unshakable spiritual significance, proclaiming that even when the world trembles in its final moments, Jagannath Dham shall remain the last refuge for true devotees. It is said that a great secret lies beneath the temple, hidden from the eyes of the world, waiting to reveal itself when the time is right.

The Disguised Devotees: The Silent Pillars of Dharma

In an age where deception runs rampant, true devotees are often unseen, living under the guise of commoners. This scripture identifies them as the torchbearers of divine wisdom, silently working to uphold dharma amid the chaos of Kali Yuga. Saints, sages, and even divine beings walk unnoticed, ensuring that faith never perishes.

The Timeless Leelas of Sri Krishna: Dwapara's Connection to Kali Yuga

The manuscript makes a profound connection between the past and present, asserting that Sri Krishna's pastimes (*leelas*) in Dwapara Yuga hold clues to the mysteries of Kali Yuga. Every event of the past is said to repeat in a different form, ensuring that divine justice prevails across ages.

The Fated Predictions: Jagannath Temple and Maa Biraja Temple

Among its many revelations, the text foretells significant events concerning Jagannath Temple and Maa Biraja Temple. It speaks of divine interventions, shifts in power, and the eventual restoration of their true essence. The verses hint at events that will shake the faith of millions but ultimately reaffirm the indestructibility of *dharma*.

The Significance of Meena Shani: Saturn's Final Omen

A critical celestial marker discussed in this text is the transit of Shani (Saturn) in Meena Rashi (Pisces). This planetary alignment is described as a harbinger of great changes—political shifts, natural upheavals, and the awakening of hidden forces. It is said that when Meena Shani reaches its peak, the final chapters of Kali Yuga shall unfold, bringing forth the last cycle of justice before the world resets.

Conclusion: The Prophecies Await Their Time

The *Bhavishyata Parardha* is not just a manuscript; it is a bridge between the seen and the unseen, the past and the future. It warns, it guides, and it prepares those who seek the truth. As the world hurtles towards its destined fate, these words stand as an eternal beacon for those who wish to understand the cosmic play of time and divinity.

For those with the wisdom to decode its secrets, the path is illuminated. For those who turn away, time itself shall be the greatest revealer.

CHAPTER 11

SUNYA SANHITA - THE MYSTICAL PROPHECIES OF MAHAPURUSA ACHYUTANANDA DAS

Odia Verse:

"ତୁମ୍ଭେ ମୋର ପଞ୍ଚ ଆମ୍ଭା। ଅଟ ପଞ୍ଚ ଜଣ । ଅବତାର ଶ୍ରେଣୀ ଯେତେ ତୁୟ ପାଇଁ ଶୁଣ । ଯାଅ ଅଚ୍ୟୁତ ଅନନ୍ତ ଯଶୋବନ୍ତ ଦାସ । ବଳରାମ ଜଗନ୍ନାଥ କର ଯେ ପ୍ରକାଶ ।"

- ଶୂନ୍ୟ ସଂହିତା

English Translation:

"You are my five eternal souls, the five divine ones. All incarnations manifest for you — listen, O sons. Go forth, Achyuta, Ananta, Jasobanta, Balarama, Jagannatha — let your divine light surpass."

- *Sunya Sanhita*

Odia Verse:

"ଶ୍ରୀ କୃଷ୍ଣ ଚରଣେ ଚିତ୍ତ ନିବେଶିବ ଯେବେ । ମନର ନିଶ୍ଚଳ ଭକ୍ତି ପ୍ରକାଶିବ ତେବେ ।"

- ଶୂନ୍ୟ ସଂହିତା, ଷଷ୍ଠ ଅଧ୍ୟାୟ

English Translation:

"When the mind surrenders at shri krishna's feet, true unwavering devotion shall be complete."

- Sunya Sanhita, 6th Chapter

Unveiling the Cosmic Secrets of Sunya Sanhita

Hidden within the prophetic traditions of Bhavishya Malika lies an esoteric manuscript—Sunya Sanhita, authored by the revered Saint Achyutananda Das. Unlike conventional Scriptures, Sunya Sanhita is a gateway to profound spiritual mysteries, cosmic revelations, and the ultimate truths about existence. Through this text, Mahapurusa Achyutananda Das deciphers the nature of Parambrahma, the origin of divine wisdom, and the role of sacred mantras in transcending material illusion.

The Cosmic Secrets of Parambrahma Jagannath

At the heart of Sunya Sanhita is the realization that the Supreme Consciousness (Parambrahma), often identified with Lord Jagannath, is beyond form and perception. The text describes Sunya Brahma—the infinite void that is neither nothingness nor existence but the essence of all creation.

Mahapurusa Achyutananda explains how the universe is a projection of this infinite void and how everything, from celestial bodies to human souls, emerges and dissolves within this eternal source.

This philosophy aligns with the core teachings of Bhavishya Malika, emphasizing that Mahaprabhu Jagannath is not merely an idol or deity but the eternal, formless consciousness that governs creation.

The Origin of Panchasakha Tatva

Mahapurusa Achyutananda Das describes the divine purpose behind the formation of the Panchasakha—the five enlightened sages (Achyutananda, Balaram Das, Jagannath Das, Jasobanta Das, and Ananta Das). He explains that they were divinely chosen to spread esoteric wisdom and guide humanity through the trials of Kali Yuga.

According to Sunya Sanhita, the Panchasakha are the carriers of eternal truth, reincarnations of celestial beings sent to prepare the world for cosmic transformation. Each of them was bestowed with divine knowledge and unique revelations about the future of mankind.

The Role and Significance of Chaitanya Mahaprabhu

Sunya Sanhita acknowledges the crucial role of Chaitanya Mahaprabhu, the divine Saint regarded as an incarnation of Lord Jagannath himself. Mahapurusa Achyutananda describes

Chaitanya Mahaprabhu as a divine reformer who revived the lost path of Bhakti Yoga—pure devotion to the Supreme Being.

The text emphasizes that Chaitanya Mahaprabhu's movement was not just about religious chanting but a cosmic intervention designed to counteract the spiritual decline of Kali Yuga. His propagation of the Hare Krishna Mahamantra is portrayed as the key to liberation, with Sunya Sanhita reinforcing its potency in awakening the soul.

The Five Core Wisdoms:

Sunya Sanhita introduces five fundamental aspects of spiritual wisdom:

1. **Sarira Tatva** – The knowledge of the body and its connection to the cosmos.
2. **Nama Tatva** – The power of divine names (Nama Sankirtan) as the easiest path to liberation.
3. **Guru Tatva** – The significance of a true spiritual teacher (Sadguru) in guiding seekers to truth.
4. **Hari-Hara Tatva** – The unity of Vishnu (Hari) and Shiva (Hara), breaking sectarian divisions.
5. **Radha-Krishna Tatva** – The mystical love of Radha and Krishna as the highest form of divine union, beyond material duality.

These principles form the core spiritual foundation necessary to overcome the illusions of Maya and attain divine realization.

The Power of Mantras:

The final revelation of Sunya Sanhita concerns the transformative power of sacred sound vibrations. Mahapurusa Achyutananda explains three primary mantras that hold immense spiritual power:

1. **Mahamantra** – The "Hare Rama Hare Krishna" or "Hare Krishna Hare Rama" chant, which purifies the mind and soul.
2. **Ekakshara Mantra** – The single-syllable mantra (ॐ), symbolizing the absolute reality.
3. **Anakshara Mantra** – The unspoken, eternal sound beyond human comprehension, leading to direct realization of Sunya Brahma.

These mantras are described as the ultimate tools to transcend the limitations of material existence and attain self-realization.

Conclusion: The Relevance of Sunya Sanhita in Today's World

Despite being written centuries ago, Sunya Sanhita remains incredibly relevant in modern times. As humanity faces increasing chaos, moral decline, and spiritual disconnection, Saint Achyutananda's prophecies remind us that true liberation lies in seeking the eternal truth beyond illusion.

The manuscript is not just a historical relic—it is a living guide for those who wish to prepare for the spiritual transformation. Through the wisdom of Sunya Sanhita, seekers can understand the cosmic order, embrace divine consciousness, and navigate the unfolding events of Kali Yuga with clarity and devotion as well as embark on an inner journey—a path toward transcending material illusions and realizing the ultimate truth hidden within the void of existence.

CHAPTER 12

CHUMBAKA MALIKA - THE DIVINE SECRETS OF KALI YUGA

Odia Verse:

"ବିଷାକ୍ତ ପବନ ବହିବ ଗହନ ଆସକ୍ତ ଲୋକ ହୋଇବେ ।
ବିଷାକ୍ତ ପବନ ବହିବ ଭୁବନ ପାପୀମାନେ ନଷ୍ଟ ହେବେ ।
କାନ୍ତାନୀ ଗୁପ୍ତେ ଭ୍ରମଣ କରିବେ ମାରୁତ ରୂପେ ବହିବେ ।
ଯୋଗୀଗଣ ସବୁ ଏକାଠି ବୁଲିଣ ଦ୍ୱାରେ ଦ୍ୱାରେ ଯେ ମିଳିବେ ।"
              - ଚୁମ୍ୟକ ମାଳିକା, ପ୍ରଥମ ଅଧ୍ୟାୟ

English Translation:

"Poisonous winds shall blow, and people will fall ill, The cursed breeze shall consume the world at will. The sinners will perish in this dreadful tide, As divine yoginis move, unseen, far and wide. Shifting like winds, they will silently sweep, Reaching every soul, in shadows deep."
              - Chumbaka Malika, 1st Chapter

Odia Verse:

"ହିନ୍ଦୁ ଧର୍ମ ଛାଡି ଥୋକେ ଯବନ ଧର୍ମରେ । ମ୍ଳେଚ୍ଛ କର୍ମ ଆଚରିବେ ମ୍ଳେଚ୍ଛ ସଙ୍ଗତରେ । ପିତା ପୁତ୍ର ଗୁରୁ ଶିଷ୍ୟ ଧର୍ମ ଯେ ପାଳନ । ନ ରହିବ ବର୍ଣ୍ଣ ଚିହ୍ନ ନ ରହିବ ଧର୍ମ ଧ୍ୟାନ ।"

— ଚୁମ୍ବକ ମାଳିକା, ଦ୍ୱିତୀୟ ଅଧ୍ୟାୟ

English Translation:

"Abandoning dharma, some will stray, embracing foreign paths along the way. With mlecchas, they'll indulge in impure deeds, Forsaking the roots from which virtue feeds. Father and son, guru and disciple too, None will uphold what once was true. Lineage lost and dharma betrayed, In darkness and chaos, morals will fade."

— *Chumbaka Malika, 2nd Chapter*

The Mysteries of Chumbaka Malika

Among the most mysterious and profound revelations in the *Bhavishya Malika* scriptures, *Chumbaka Malika* stands as an extraordinary prophecy, originally narrated by Lord Vishnu to his divine carrier, Garuda. This sacred knowledge was later divinely received by the great seer Sisu Ananta Das and recorded by his devoted disciple, Baranga Das. It is said that this manuscript contains esoteric wisdom that unveils the deepest secrets of *Kali Yuga*, the final age of darkness and transformation.

The Restoration of Dharma: The Divine Play of Kalki & Baladev

The prophecies within *Chumbaka Malika* foretell the grand re-establishment of *dharma* through the divine interventions of *Baladev* and *Kalki Avatar*. As the world spirals into chaos, these two supreme beings will manifest their *leelas* (divine pastimes) to cleanse of its impurities. Baladev, the eternal elder brother of Lord Krishna, will take a firm stand against the rising unrighteousness, while Kalki will wield the ultimate weapon of divine judgment, ensuring that the era of falsehood meets its destined end.

The Warriors of Dharma: Devotees Who Will Assist Kalki Avatar

The scripture speaks of select groups of devoted souls who will incarnate with the sole purpose of aiding Kalki Avatar in his mission. These beings, born under divine influence, will possess unwavering faith and extraordinary abilities. Though hidden among ordinary mortals, they will rise at the destined time, revealing their true purpose in the cosmic battle between righteousness and sin. They will recognize each other not by appearance but by the fire of devotion burning in their hearts.

The Divine Mysteries of the 64 Yoginis

The *Chumbaka Malika* delves deep into the mystical *leela* of the 64 Yoginis, celestial female energies who embody supreme power. These Yoginis will manifest in *Kali Yuga* to restore cosmic balance, acting as protectors of sacred wisdom. Their presence will be felt in unseen ways, guiding the chosen ones toward the path of truth.

Mahamaya: The Mother of the Cosmos

At the heart of these divine interventions stands Mahamaya, the supreme cosmic mother. Her power transcends all dimensions, controlling both the illusory and the real. The scripture speaks of her unseen influence, orchestrating the destruction of evil while nurturing the seeds of dharma. Though hidden from the eyes of the unworthy, those with pure hearts will feel her guiding presence in the darkest of times.

The Corruption of Humanity: Traits of a Kali-Influenced Being

A grim warning is given about the characteristics of humans consumed by the influence of *Kali Yuga*. These individuals will be driven by material greed, lust, and deception. Their devotion will be false, their words laced with deceit, and their actions guided by selfishness. The sacred text paints a picture of a world where virtue is abandoned for temporary pleasure, where even the most sacred relationships—father and son, guru and disciple—will be broken by betrayal and dishonor.

The Hidden and Unknown "Sisu Veda"

One of the most astonishing revelations of *Chumbaka Malika* is the existence of an unknown and concealed scripture called Sisu Veda. Unlike the four well-known Vedas, this ancient text holds secrets that were deliberately hidden from the corrupted minds of *Kali Yuga*. It is said that only the most enlightened souls will have access to its wisdom, as its knowledge is not meant for the impure.

The Sins of Kali Yuga: Humanity's Self-Destruction

The manuscript provides a detailed account of the heinous sins that will plague humanity in *Kali Yuga*. Deception, unrestrained desires, betrayal, and cruelty will become commonplace. The once-holy lands will be tainted with bloodshed, and those who once walked the path of righteousness will be lured into the shadows of evil. False prophets will arise, leading millions astray, and even the holiest of places will not be spared from desecration.

Gupta Khandagiri (Jaluka Hills): The Secret Sanctuary of Divine Energies

The text reveals the hidden significance of Gupta Khandagiri (Jaluka Hills, Odisha), a mystical location where divine forces are believed to reside. This sacred place holds untold secrets and treasures, both material and spiritual. Those who seek the truth with a pure heart may find enlightenment here, while those who come with greed shall leave empty-handed.

Ancient Treasures: The Hidden Legacies of the Past

The prophecies also speak of hidden ancient treasures buried deep within the land, protected by divine forces. These are not just material riches but spiritual legacies—forgotten relics, sacred texts, and celestial artifacts that hold immense power. In the final days of *Kali Yuga*, these treasures will reveal themselves only to the worthy, playing a crucial role in the restoration of dharma.

The Dark Future: Diseases, Natural Disasters, and Wars

The *Chumbaka Malika* warns of catastrophic events—plagues consume millions, unseen illnesses that will baffle even the greatest healers, earthquakes that will shatter civilizations, and violent storms that will reshape the lands. War shall break out in every corner of the world, not for justice, but for greed and destruction.

Conclusion: A Warning and a Promise

The *Chumbaka Malika* is more than a prophecy—it is a mirror reflecting both the horrors of *Kali Yuga* and the hope of redemption. It warns of destruction but also reassures that *dharma* will triumph in the end. Those who remain steadfast in faith and truth will find refuge in the divine.

The storm is near, but so is salvation. The choice lies in our hands—shall we walk the path of light, or shall we be consumed by darkness?

The fate of the world awaits.

CHAPTER 13

SHIVA KALPA - THE PROPHECIES OF SAINT ACHYUTANANDA DAS

Odia Verse:

"ଶିବକଳ୍ପ ବାଣୀ ନିର୍ଘଣ୍ଟ ଶବଦେ ହେତୁ ରଖୁଥାଅ ରାମ ।
ଯେଉଁଦିନ ଏହା ପ୍ରତ୍ୟକ୍ଷ ଫଳିବ ବୁଝିବୁ ଏହାର ମର୍ମ ।"
- ଶିବକଳ୍ପ, ପଞ୍ଚଦଶ ନିର୍ଘଣ୍ଟ

English Translation:

"O Ram, keep the words of Shiva in mind,
as their true meaning will reveal at the right time."
- Shiva Kalpa, 5th Chapter

Odia Verse:

"ଘୋର କଳିକାଳ ଥୟ ନ ରହିବ ପ୍ରାଣୀ ହେବେ କୁଆ ବୁଆ ।
ପୂର୍ବ ସମୁଦ୍ରୁ ଲବଣ ଉଠିବ କମ୍ପିବ ପ୍ରାଣୀଙ୍କ ହିଆ ।"
- ଶିବକଳ୍ପ, ସପ୍ତମ ନିର୍ଘଣ୍ଟ

English Translation:

"In the dreadful Kali Yuga's reign, no soul shall live in peace again. From the eastern sea, the waves will rise, and fear will fill all hearts and eyes."

- Shiva Kalpa, 7th Chapter

The Shiva Kalpa is one of the most significant manuscripts within the Bhavishya Malika, narrated by the great Saint Achyutananda Das and written down by his devoted disciple, Ram Das. This sacred text unveils the profound wisdom of the saint and presents a step-by-step prophecy about the decline of society, global transformations, and the ultimate resurgence of Dharma in the final phase of Kali Yuga. It serves as both a warning and a guiding light for humanity, urging people to awaken before it is too late.

The Step-by-Step Decline of Society

Saint Achyutananda meticulously describes how society will witness a gradual yet complete downfall. He reveals how humanity will stray from the path of righteousness, giving in to greed, deception, and materialistic desires. The sacred bonds of family and duty will weaken, *Dharma* will be disregarded, and humans will engage in acts of extreme selfishness, cruelty, and sin. He warns that dishonesty will be rewarded, and those who follow the path of truth will face severe struggles.

The Significance of Saturn in Pisces & Its Negative Effects

The Shiva Kalpa extensively discusses the astrological importance of Saturn's transit into Pisces (Meena Rashi), which will mark the final era of Kali Yuga. Mahapurusa Achyutananda reveals that during this period, chaos and suffering will increase. Saturn, the great karmic judge, will unleash its full influence, causing widespread despair, economic downfall, and natural disasters. It will serve as a time of purification, where only the righteous will endure the turbulence.

Global Warming, Climate Change & Catastrophes

Long before modern science raised alarms, Shiva Kalpa predicted the devastating effects of climate change. Saint Achyutananda foresaw that humanity's unchecked greed and exploitation of nature would lead to severe environmental crises. Rising temperatures, melting ice caps, and unprecedented storms will result in mass destruction, leading to the loss of countless lives and the submergence of entire countries. He warns that this will be nature's response to mankind's sins, urging people to return to a harmonious existence with the environment.

Specific Astrological Events That Will Mark the End Times

The manuscript describes celestial alignments that will indicate the nearing end of Kali Yuga. The movement of planets, eclipses, and rare planetary conjunctions will serve as divine warnings. Mahapurusa Achyutananda speaks of a time when the Sun and

Moon will lose their brilliance, and the stars will behave erratically, causing global panic. He stresses that those who understand these cosmic messages will prepare for the great transition.

The Birth of Great Saints & Sages in Every Yuga

Saint Achyutananda highlights the role of divine beings in each era. He mentions that every *Yuga* witnesses the birth of Mahapurushas (great souls), Rishi Munis (sages), and Sadhus (Saints) who work to guide humanity. These enlightened beings take birth at crucial moments to protect *Dharma* and uplift the fallen souls. However, in Kali Yuga, such saints will often be ridiculed and ignored by the ignorant masses.

Major Global Events That Will Reshape Humanity

The Shiva Kalpa contains extraordinary predictions about pivotal global events. Some of the most striking ones include:

- A great war in Mecca-Madina, signaling a turning point in global geopolitics.
- The submergence of the sacred Puri Jagannath Temple in the sea, an event marking the final phase of Kali Yuga.
- Conflicts and uprisings that will shift the balance of power among nations.
- Natural disasters that will wipe out corrupt civilizations while sparing the land of Dharma.

The Birth of Abhiram Paramahansa: The Divine Guide

Among the many prophecies in Shiva Kalpa, one of the most fascinating is the foretold birth of a great Saint named Abhiram Paramahansa. This enlightened soul will emerge to guide humanity in its darkest times, imparting divine wisdom and leading seekers toward truth. His presence will serve as a beacon of hope, gathering followers from all corners of the world who seek spiritual salvation.

The Devotees & Their Countries of Birth

The manuscript reveals the rebirth of many devoted souls across different nations. Mahapurusa Achyutananda provides intricate details about where these bhaktas (devotees) will be born, their spiritual duties, and how they will play a role in the grand divine plan. He emphasizes that true seekers will recognize each other, forming a spiritual network to withstand the coming tribulations.

The Role of Kalki & Balaram in Re-establishing Dharma

As Kali Yuga reaches its peak of darkness, the forces of righteousness will rise. Mahapurusa Achyutananda describes the divine mission of Lord Kalki, the prophesied tenth incarnation of Lord Vishnu, who will descend to vanquish evil and restore *Dharma*. Alongside him, Lord Balaram will take his rightful place as the ruler of the new world order. Their arrival will signal the ultimate destruction of *Adharma* and the rebirth of an age of truth.

The Call to Awaken: Preparing for a New Age of Truth

The final message of Shiva Kalpa is a powerful call to humanity. Mahapurusa Achyutananda urges people to realize the illusion of Kali Yuga—a time dominated by falsehood, deception, and suffering. He advises all seekers to prepare for the transition into a new era by cultivating Bhakti (devotion), embracing spirituality, and rejecting the false narratives of this dark age.

Conclusion

The Shiva Kalpa is not just a collection of prophecies—it is a divine roadmap for those seeking to navigate the chaos of Kali Yuga. It unveils the hidden truths about the world's downfall, the role of celestial events, the resurgence of great saints, and the final battle for *Dharma*. In the midst of destruction, it offers hope, reminding humanity that after the storm, the dawn of a new age of truth and righteousness awaits.

CHAPTER 14

JAIPHULA MALIKA - THE PROPHECIES OF MAHAPURUSA ACHYUTANANDA

Odia Verse:

"ଟାଣ କରି କହୁଥିବେ ଯେଉଁ ଭକ୍ତମାନେ । ଟଳ ଟଳ ହୋଇବେ କଳ୍କୀ ଆଗମନେ । ଟାକିଅଛି ମହାମାୟୀ ଖପର ପତାଇ । ଟାଣ ଭାଙ୍ଗି ଦେବ ଦୀନ ଅଚ୍ୟୁତ କହଇ ।"
— ଜାଇଫୁଲ ମାଲିକା, ପ୍ରଥମ ଅଧ୍ୟାୟ

English Translation:

"The wicked and blind, consumed by pride, shall tremble in fear when Kalki arrives. Goddess Mahamaya awaits the hour, to shatter each ego with divine power."
— Jaiphula Malika, 1st Chapter

Odia Verse:

"ପଥେ ଏଣେ ରାତ୍ର ଦିବା ଯୁଦ୍ଧ ଯେ ଲାଗିବ । ପ୍ରସ୍ତାବିତ କଳି ମହାଭାରତ ହୋଇବ ।"

— ଜାଇଫୁଲ ମାଳିକା, ପ୍ରଥମ ଅଧ୍ୟାୟ

English Translation:

"Wars will rage, both day and night, as Kali Yuga's Mahabharata ignites the fight."

— *Jaiphula Malika, 1st Chapter*

The *Jaiphula Malika* is a rare and invaluable manuscript within the *Bhavishya Malika*, containing an intense and enlightening conversation between the great Saint Achyutananda Das and his foremost disciple, Ram Das. This manuscript provides a deep insight into the unfolding of Kali Yuga, the final age of darkness, and reveals extraordinary prophecies concerning the end times, the arrival of Kalki Avatar, the rebirth of great warriors, and the restoration of Dharma.

The Divine Conversation Between Mahapurusa Achyutananda & Ram Das

This manuscript is a recorded dialogue where Ram Das, filled with curiosity, questions his revered guru, Saint Achyutananda Das, about the fate of the world, his own future births, and the destiny of Bharata Varsha. Mahapurusa Achyutananda, in his infinite wisdom, answers with precise details, offering both warnings and hope for the seekers of truth.

Mahapurusa Achyutananda's Final Birth in Kali Yuga

One of the most intriguing revelations in the *Jaiphula Malika* is Saint Achyutananda's declaration regarding his final and 13th birth in Kali Yuga. He not only confirms his rebirth but also provides precise landmarks and geographical identifiers to locate his presence. This revelation serves as a guiding light for true seekers to find the divine reincarnation of the Saint in these tumultuous times.

The True Age of Kali Yuga: 5000 Years

Contrary to the popular belief that Kali Yuga spans 4,32,000 years, Mahapurusa Achyutananda reveals that its actual duration is merely 5,000 years. He explains that human perception of time has been distorted, and the final dissolution will arrive much sooner than expected. This radical prediction urges mankind to awaken and prepare for the ultimate transition.

Prophecies on Decline of Dharma & Society

The *Jaiphula Malika* forewarns of a severe decline in Dharma, morality, and ethical values. Saint Achyutananda describes how greed, lust, and deception will dominate human hearts, leading to widespread corruption, pollution, and natural calamities. The once-sacred rivers will turn poisonous, the air will be thick with impurities, and people will abandon righteousness for materialistic gains.

Wars & Conflicts in the End Times

The manuscript describes multiple devastating wars that will take place before the Kali Yuga ends. These wars, both external and internal, will be fought between the forces of righteousness and darkness. Mahapurusa Achyutananda emphasizes that only those who remain steadfast in their spiritual path will survive the impending chaos.

Visible Signs of the End Times

Saint Achyutananda provides a detailed list of visible signs that will appear as Kali Yuga approaches its final moments. He describes natural disasters, cosmic disturbances, and social unrest as indicators of the nearing end. The division between good and evil will become increasingly clear, and those who walk the path of truth will be called to fulfill their divine roles.

Illegal Immigrants & the Unrest in Bharata

A controversial yet profound prophecy in the *Jaiphula Malika* discusses the influx of illegal immigrants in Bharata Varsha. Saint Achyutananda warns that these individuals will disrupt the harmony of the land through their wicked deeds, creating unrest and suffering. Yet, he also foretells their destined path, envisioning a divine harmony that will renew the sanctity of the land.

Rebirth of Pandavas & Kauravas in Kali Yuga

The manuscript reveals that the legendary warriors of the *Mahabharata*—the Pandavas and the Kauravas—have reincarnated in Kali Yuga with specific duties assigned to them. Mahapurusa Achyutananda details their exact whereabouts, their hidden identities, and the roles they will play in the modern-day battle of righteousness.

The Rise of Lord Balaram as the Ruler of Earth

A significant prophecy within *Jaiphula Malika* is the rise of Lord Balaram (Baladev), who will emerge as the supreme ruler of the planet. His reign will mark the return of Dharma and spiritual purity, restoring the lost glory of Sanatana Dharma.

The Meeting of Kalki & Balaram

Saint Achyutananda describes the momentous meeting between Lord Kalki and Lord Balaram. This meeting will take place at a predestined location, where they will discuss strategies to cleanse the world of evil and establish a new spiritual order. This prophecy hints at the grand divine plan that will unfold in the final phase of Kali Yuga.

Chhatia Leela: The Final Play of Lord Jagannath

The *Jaiphula Malika* also describes the *Chhatia Leela*, the ultimate divine play of Lord Jagannath in Kali Yuga. It is prophesied that Lord Jagannath will perform his final *Leela* in Chhatia, marking the culmination of his presence in this age and the ushering in of a new cosmic cycle.

The Power of Rama Tatva & the Path to Salvation

Saint Achyutananda emphasizes the significance of *Rama Tatva*—the essence of Lord Rama—and the chanting of *Rama Nama* as the supreme path to salvation. He assures that even in the darkest times, the pure devotion to *Rama Nama* can liberate the soul from the cycle of birth and death.

The Ultimate Call for Bhakti & Spiritual Awakening

In his concluding words, Mahapurusa Achyutananda urges humanity to embrace *Bhakti* and spirituality as the only means to transcend the suffering of Kali Yuga. He calls upon all seekers to walk the path of truth, righteousness, and divine wisdom, for the ultimate battle between Dharma and Adharma is near.

Conclusion

The *Jaiphula Malika* stands as a sacred testament to the cosmic plan of Kali Yuga. It is both a warning and a guide for those who seek the truth. The manuscript's revelations about end times, the rise of Kalki Avatar, and the restoration of Dharma serve as a beacon of hope for all spiritual seekers. Mahapurusa Achyutananda Das, through his timeless wisdom, provides humanity with the knowledge and the path to transcend the darkness and enter a new divine era.

CHAPTER 15

KAALA NIRGHANTA - THE TIMELINES OF DESTINY

Odia Verse:

"ଶୁଣ ରାମଦାସ ତୁହି ହେତୁ କରି ଘେନ । ମହା ଶବଦ ଶୁଣିଶ ନିସ୍ତାର ପ୍ରମାଣ । ଭକ୍ତମାନଙ୍କୁ କଷ୍ଟ ବହୁତ ହେବାରୁ । ଡାକ ଶୁଣି, ନୀଳକନ୍ଧୁ ଆସି ମହାମେରୁ ।"

— କାଳ ନିର୍ଘଣ୍ଟ, ତୃତୀୟ ସୁରସ

English Translation:

"O Rama Das, hear and see, these are the words that set souls free. Devotees shall suffer, burdened with pain, but Jagannath shall come at their call again."

— Kala Nirghanta, 3rd Chapter

Odia Verse:

"ନିଶାରେ ଯେ ଜନମାନେ ଶୟନରେ ଥିବେ । ରାତ୍ରି ଯେ ପାହିଲେ ସତ୍ୟବଚନ କହିବେ । ସତ୍ୟ କଳି ପ୍ରବେଶ ଜାଣିବୁ ସତ୍ୟ ସର୍ବ । ପ୍ରଭୁଙ୍କର ଆଜ୍ଞା ସେ ଯେ ମେଣ୍ଢଣ ହୋଇବ ।"

— କାଳ ନିର୍ଘଣ୍ଟ, ପଞ୍ଚମ ସୁରସ

English Translation:

"On the final night, the sleeping shall stay unaware, and with the sunrise, truth they will declare. Before this begins, Satya-Kali will unfold, by Lord's command, Satya Yuga shall take hold."

- Kala Nirghanta, 5th Chapter

Among the many divine revelations bestowed upon the great seer Achyutananda Das, *Kaala Nirghanta* stands as a celestial roadmap of time itself. This manuscript, narrated by Mahapurusa Achyutananda Das and meticulously recorded by his devoted disciple Rama Das, unveils the hidden currents of fate that will shape the final epoch of Kali Yuga and herald the arrival of a new age. It does not merely foretell events—it dictates the rhythm of cosmic justice, where greed, war, and calamities shall pave the way for the rise of divine order.

The Decline of Society: Greed, Wars, and Calamities

The prophecy begins with a chilling portrayal of Kali Yuga's darkest hours. Saint Achyutananda Das warns that society will descend into chaos, driven by the unchecked greed of men. False leaders will rise, righteousness will fade, and the innocent will suffer at the hands of the corrupt. As a consequence, natural disasters will strike with fury—earthquakes will shatter great cities, floods will drown entire civilizations, and relentless droughts will scorch the earth. Wars will erupt not for justice but for power, turning Bharat into a battlefield where dharma shall be tested one last time.

The Arrival of Kalki: The Final Avatar of Lord Vishnu

In the midst of this destruction, the prophecy reveals a glimmer of divine intervention—the coming of Kalki Avatar, the final incarnation of Lord Vishnu. Unlike other avatars, whose presence was known to the world, Kalki shall walk unseen, preparing in secrecy. Only the most devoted souls shall recognize his signs, while the ignorant masses will reject him until it is too late. The scriptures describe him as the wielder of a blazing sword, mounted upon a celestial horse, destined to cleanse the world of its impurities.

The First Kalki Temple: Chhatia's Mystical Significance

The text shines a divine light upon the Chhatia Temple, the first-ever shrine dedicated to Kalki Avatar, established by the enlightened Saint Hadi Das—the twelfth birth of Saint Achyutananda Das himself. This temple is not just a place of worship but a cosmic gateway, where the energies of the future converge with the present. It is said that when the end times approach, divine signals will manifest in this sacred site, serving as a beacon for those seeking refuge from the storm of destruction.

The Political Upheaval in Bharat: The Fall of Corrupt Rulers

The prophecy paints a turbulent picture of Bharat's political landscape in the final days of Kali Yuga. It speaks of rulers who will betray their own people, driven by lust for power and blind ambition. Bharat shall be torn apart by internal strife, its leaders puppets in the hands of dark forces. Yet, from the ashes of deception, a great transformation shall rise—an unyielding force of dharma, led by warriors destined to restore the land to its former glory.

The Dawn of Satya Yuga: The Age of Truth Returns

Beyond the trials of Kali Yuga, the prophecy reveals the emergence of a new golden age—Satya Yuga, the Age of Truth. In this era, humanity will be reborn in its purest form, free from the chains of materialism and deception. The earth shall heal, and righteousness will once again reign supreme. The wicked shall be no more, and only those with unwavering devotion shall step into the divine light of the new era.

The Final War of Kali Yuga: The Battlefield of Bharat

Before the transition to Satya Yuga, one last war must be fought—the final battle of Kali Yuga, waged upon the sacred soil of Bharat. This war shall not be fought with mere weapons but with the forces of karma itself. The righteous shall rise against the forces of darkness, and dharma shall wield its final judgement. This battle is the culmination of ages, where those who have upheld truth shall emerge victorious, while the deceitful shall perish in the fire of divine retribution.

The Hidden Rishis, Munis, and Yogis: Guardians of the Eternal Wisdom

While the world suffers the consequences of its own misdeeds, a hidden network of enlightened beings continues to protect the sacred wisdom of the past. The Kaala Nirghanta speaks of Rishis, Munis, and Yogis who remain alive, secluded in mystical caves and undiscovered sanctuaries, meditating for the right moment to reveal themselves. They hold the lost knowledge of the universe, waiting for the day when humanity is ready to receive it once more.

Conclusion: The Fate of the World Lies in These Prophecies

The Kaala Nirghanta is not merely a manuscript—it is a celestial warning, a divine prophecy, and an unchangeable decree of time itself. It does not merely predict the fall of Kali Yuga but offers a path of salvation for those who choose to walk in the light of dharma.

It reminds us that no matter how dark the night may become, the dawn of truth shall always rise.

The battle lines are drawn, and destiny awaits. The question remains—are you prepared to witness the unfolding of fate?

CHAPTER 16

THE HIDDEN MEANING OF NUMBERS, YEARS & CODES

Odia Verse:

"ଠାରେ ଠାରେ ବସା ଅଙ୍କ ସାଲ ମାନ । ମନ୍ତ୍ର ଯନ୍ତ୍ର ତନ୍ତ୍ର ଯେତକ ଭାନ ।ସବୁ ଲେଖାଠାରେ ଠାର ବସାଇ । ଯେ ବୁଝିବ ସେହି ଭକ୍ତ ଅଟଇ ।"

— ଅଚ୍ୟୁତାନନ୍ଦ ଦାସ, ଭବିଷ୍ୟତ ପରାର୍ଦ୍ଧ, ପ୍ରଥମ ପରାର୍ଦ୍ଧ

English Translation:

"At various places, the numerical figures are set. Mantras, Yantras, and Tantras—whatever is known. Everything is inscribed and placed in its position. Only those who understand have true devotion."

— Achyutanand Das, Bhavishyata Parardha, 1st Parardha

Throughout the ages, the revered Panchasakha have employed a unique system of calculations to predict the exact timeline of significant global events mentioned in Bhavishya Malika. Their methodology revolves around three core elements: Anka (Numbers), Sala (Years), and Thara Gara (Codes with Hidden

Meaning). While many researchers attempted to decode these intricate predictions, they often miscalculated, leading to false dates and misinterpretations. However, after a decade-long dedicated study of the original manuscripts, I have been able to uncover some of the hidden meanings.

Secrets of Anka (Numbers)

The Panchasakha utilized numerical values to pinpoint the exact timeline of major world-altering events such as wars, natural calamities, economic crisis, and political upheavals. These numbers hold a sacred connection with three primary temples:

- **Jagannath Temple** (*Gajapati Anka*)
- **Maa Biraja Temple** (*Biraja Anka*)
- **Chhatia Temple** (*Chhatia Anka*)

Each year, on specific tithis (lunar phases), these numbers undergo an ascending transformation, altering their prophetic significance. These changes provide a cryptic yet precise indications of forthcoming events.

Secrets of Sala (Years)

The concept of Sala refers to the chronological framework used by the Panchasakha to determine the timing of crucial predictions. They referenced various traditional Hindu calendars (Panchang) to align their prophecies with specific time periods. These included:

- Jagannath Panchang
- Biraja Panchang
- Saka Panchang
- Vikram Samvat Panchang
- Kaliyuga Panchang

By meticulously analyzing these calendars, they were able to foretell global shifts and upheavals with remarkable precision.

Secrets of Thara Gara (Hidden Codes)

A deeper layer of the Panchasakha's predictive system lies within Thara Gara—a series of coded messages used to disguise the true meaning of their prophecies. These codes are rooted in three fundamental disciplines:

1. **Jyotish Shastra (Astrology)** – Aligning planetary movements with historical cycles.
2. **Mathematical Equations** – Using numerical formulas to determine the unfolding of events.
3. **Historical & Mythological Puzzles** – Concealing messages within metaphorical language and ancient symbols.

By decrypting these codes, one can uncover the hidden patterns of destiny that dictate the course of human civilization.

Conclusion: The Lost Knowledge of the Ages

The Panchasakha did not encrypt their prophecies out of secrecy but out of necessity. They knew that as Kali Yuga deepened, the world would be plagued by deception, corruption, and spiritual blindness. If this sacred knowledge were to fall into the wrong hands, it could be misused for power and manipulation.

Only those with pure intent, unwavering devotion, and deep spiritual wisdom can unlock the true meaning of Bhavishya Malika. The hidden numbers, the coded years, and the cryptic messages are not just remnants of the past—they hold the key to the future.

Now, as we stand on the threshold of great change, the question remains: Will you seek the truth hidden within these ancient codes, or will you let time slip away as destiny unfolds before your eyes?

CHAPTER 17

PROPHECIES THAT CAME TRUE

*W*hat if an ancient manuscript held the power to foresee wars, political upheavals, and disasters with chilling accuracy? The Bhavishya Malika, a mystical treasure of divine wisdom, has astounded generations with its uncanny foresight. Deciphering its enigmatic verses has long been a formidable challenge, given its ancient script and intricate language. Yet, with unwavering dedication, reverence for the wisdom of the Panchasakha, and a methodical approach, I have uncovered a series of prophecies that strikingly mirror modern events. These revelations are a testament to the divine foresight embedded within the *Bhavishya Malika*. In this chapter, I present a curated collection of predictions that have materialized, supported by factual accounts and corroborative evidence.

For more insights and extended discussions, you are invited to explore my YouTube Channel, "Viral Odisha."

Predictions Decoded and Published By Me On My YouTube Channel Before They Came True:

1. Russia's Invasion of Ukraine (2022):

Prediction: The Bhavishya Malika hinted at a major conflict beginning in 2022 involving Russia.

Outcome: On February 24, 2022, Russia initiated a full-scale invasion of Ukraine, marking a profound escalation in the regional conflict and reshaping global geopolitics.

2. Narendra Modi's Victory in the 2024 General Elections:

Prediction: The Bhavishya Malika indicated that in 2024, Narendra Modi would secure a third consecutive term as Prime Minister.

Outcome: The 2024 elections culminated in a decisive win for the NDA, confirming Modi's enduring leadership.

3. Israel's Military Engagement with Extremist Factions:

Prediction: The Bhavishya Malika foresaw a significant conflict involving Israel and extremist factions beginning in 2023.

Outcome: In 2023, Israel launched targeted military actions against extremist groups, triggering geopolitical shifts and extensive international debate.

4. Escalated Conflicts in the Red Sea Region:

Prediction: The Bhavishya Malika warned of violent confrontations in the Red Sea region emerging by 2023 - 2024.

Outcome: Throughout 2024, the region experienced intensified maritime clashes and territorial disputes, resulting in tragic casualties and heightened tensions.

5. Reinforced Immigration Policies in India:

Prediction: The Bhavishya Malika predicted that between 2024 - 2025, India would implement strict immigration policies targeting undocumented immigrants.

Outcome: During this period, stringent immigration policies were implemented to enhance national security and maintain demographic balance.

6. Reopening of the Jagannath Temple's Four Doors and Revelation of Ratna Bhandar:

Prediction: The Bhavishya Malika indicated that in 2024, all four doors of the Jagannath Temple would be reopened and the mysteries of the Ratna Bhandar (treasure chamber) would be revealed.

Outcome: In 2024, temple authorities reopened all the four doors, and the *Ratna Bhandar* was made accessible for public survey, drawing global attention and renewed devotion.

7. Political and Economic Shifts in Europe:

Prediction: The Bhavishya Malika predicted that by 2024 - 2025, Europe would face growing instability driven by demographic shifts and economic pressures.

Outcome: By 2024, Europe witnessed heightened political tensions and significant economic recalibrations, reshaping social policies across the continent.

8. Regional Instability in Bangladesh and Pakistan:

Prediction: The Bhavishya Malika warned that Bangladesh and Pakistan would face political and economic turmoil starting in 2023.

Outcome: Both nations experienced escalating internal challenges, marked by economic downturns and social unrest, leading to ongoing policy debates.

9. Unrest in Northeast India:

Prediction: The Bhavishya Malika predicted that by 2023, Northeast India would face widespread ethnic and insurgent unrest.

Outcome: Beginning in 2023, the region saw intensified conflicts and political instability, affecting development and social harmony—especially highlighted by the unfolding crisis in Manipur.

10. Food and Water Scarcity Crisis in Africa:

Prediction: The Bhavishya Malika foretold an unprecedented crisis in food and water resources across Africa, beginning in 2023.

Outcome: By 2024, several African nations grappled with severe shortages, triggering widespread humanitarian challenges and prompting urgent policy responses.

Historical Prophecies and Their Manifestations

But the Bhavishya Malika's revelations are not confined to recent events alone. Its foresight extends deep into history, chronicling pivotal moments that have shaped civilizations—proving its wisdom transcends both time and space.

1. **Mughal and British Invasions of Bharat:** The Bhavishya Malika foretold the arrival of foreign powers that would dominate the Indian subcontinent—a vision that aligns with the historical invasions and subsequent rule by the Mughal Empire and the British Raj.
2. **Rise of Netaji Subhas Chandra Bose:** The prophecies hinted at a charismatic leader destined to challenge colonial rule, a description that resonates with the life and struggles of Netaji Subhas Chandra Bose during India's fight for independence.
3. **Rise and Fall of Adolf Hitler:** Ancient verses alluded to a powerful Western leader whose actions would plunge the world into conflict, echoing Hitler's rise during World War II and his eventual downfall.
4. **Natural Calamities:** Predictions regarding events such as the 1999 Super Cyclone in Odisha, the 2004 Boxing Day Tsunami, and the COVID-19 Pandemic reflect the manuscript's foresight into disasters that reshaped societies and economies worldwide.
5. **Technological and Environmental Shifts:** The ancient texts also anticipated the rise of artificial intelligence, shifts in Earth's magnetic poles, and the unfolding climate crisis—highlighting their relevance in guiding modern policy and public discourse.

Conclusion

The Bhavishya Malika is not merely an ancient manuscript; it is a timeless compendium of prophetic wisdom that bridges the past, present, and future. Its decoded revelations, whether foretelling geopolitical conflicts, spiritual awakenings, or global shifts, serve as both a guide and a warning for humanity. As these insights continue to manifest, one undeniable truth emerges — while destiny may be foretold, our actions today hold the power to alter tomorrow.

Could this ancient manuscript be humanity's final warning — or its greatest hope? The answer lies in what we choose to do next.

Disclaimer

The prophecies and events discussed in this chapter are derived from ancient interpretations of the Bhavishya Malika. While these predictions have shown striking parallels with historical and modern occurrences, they should be regarded as insights open to interpretation rather than absolute certainties. The purpose of presenting these decoded revelations is to encourage thoughtful reflection and awareness, not to create fear or alarm. Readers are encouraged to approach this content with an open mind, understanding that prophecy is often symbolic and subject to varying interpretations.

CHAPTER 18

THE BEGINNING OF WORLD WAR 3 AND KALI YUGA MAHABHARATA

Odia Verse:

"ତୃତୀୟ ମହାସମର ରୁଷିଆ ଅଭିମୁଖେ ହେବ ।"
 - ମହାପୁରୁଷ ଅଚ୍ୟୁତାନନ୍ଦ ଦାସ

English Translation:

"Third world war will begin from the land of Russia."
 - *Mahapurusa Achyutananda Das*

One of the most critical prophecies of the Bhavishya Malika concerns World War 3 and the Kali Yuga Mahabharata. Although these wars differ in nature, they are deeply interconnected. Saint Achyutananda predicted that World War 3 would originate from Russia.

Today, with the Russia–Ukraine conflict still ongoing and Europe getting involved, many geopolitical experts believe the world is on the brink of a major global confrontation. This war will not remain confined to Ukraine—it will escalate, drawing in

Europe, the Middle East, and Asia, and involving multiple world powers.

The annexation of Crimea in 2014, NATO's expansion, rising tensions in the South China Sea, and increasing global conflicts have already set the stage. The final tipping point, however, will come when Russia forms a strategic alliance with China and several other nations, challenging Western dominance and reshaping the global order.

The Final Phase – Conflict Reaches India
Odia Verse:

"ମୀନ ଶନି ଯୁକ୍ତରେ ଥିବ । ଭାରତ ଲଢ଼େଇ ହେବ ।"
- ମହାପୁରୁଷ ଅଚ୍ୟୁତାନନ୍ଦ ଦାସ

English Translation:

"When Saturn will enter Pisces, the great war will begin in Bharata."
- Mahapurusa Achyutananda Das

After the Western powers weaken, Russia is predicted to withdraw from active conflict, while China and other rival nations will shift their focus to Bharata (India).

Trigger of the War:

- **Economic Competition:** India's rapid rise as a global power will unsettle certain nations, leading to diplomatic and military tensions.

- **Geopolitical Realignments:** Shifting alliances and border disputes will intensify friction in South Asia.

The Sudden Attack:

- The conflict will begin unexpectedly from the northern borders, catching many off guard.
- India will suffer initial setbacks due to the surprise nature of the attack.

India's Role:

- Initially, India will act as a peace mediator, striving to de-escalate global tensions.
- As the war intensifies, India will be forced to take up arms to defend its sovereignty.

The Weapons of Apocalypse

Mahapurusa Achyutananda's prophecies suggest that advanced weaponry, unlike anything seen before, will be unleashed during this war. These include:

- **AI-Powered Warfare & Cyber-Based Defense Systems:** Military technology will be heavily automated, leading to unprecedented strategic battles.
- **Nuclear & Advanced Missile Technology:** Certain global powers will resort to extreme measures, resulting in devastating consequences.

- **Ancient Astras (Divine Weapons):** The Bhavishya Malika mentions that long-lost celestial weapons, hidden in sacred locations, will resurface during this conflict.

Kali Yuga Mahabharata – The Unfinished Battle

According to the *Panchasakha*, the war of Mahabharata in *Dwapara Yuga* never truly ended; its final chapter is yet to be fought—this will occur in *Kali Yuga,* on the very soil of Bharata. Mahapurusa Achyutananda prophesied that several warriors from the Mahabharata era have reincarnated in the modern world to fulfill their final karma.

The Warriors of the Final War:

- **Ashwatthama** – The immortal warrior cursed to roam the earth, destined to fulfill his final role.
- **Bhurishrava** – The fallen hero who once fought for the Kauravas but now faces a choice between redemption and ruin.
- **Karna** – The tragic warrior, torn between loyalty and destiny, returns to face his unfinished fate.
- **Shalya** – The master strategist, whose mind can turn the tide of war.
- **Ghatotkacha** – The mighty half-demon warrior, returning with unmatched strength.
- **Babruvahana** – The valiant son of Arjuna, born to carry his father's unfinished legacy.
- **Belalasena** – The silent yet powerful warrior, destined to protect Dharma.

- **Abhimanyu** – The young lion-hearted hero, returning to finish the battle he once fell in.
- **The Pandavas & Kauravas** – Divided once again—some walking the path of Dharma, while others fall prey to Adharma.

The Rise of Kalki Avatar & the Final Battles

The prophecies indicate that during this great war, Kalki and Balaram will be revealed in Odisha by enlightened Saints. They will assemble 12 commanders to form a divine army that will play a decisive role in the conflict.

Two Great Battles of Kali Yuga Mahabharata

- **Battle of the North:** Naga Sadhus will play a crucial role, fighting alongside the forces of Dharma.
- **Battle of the East:** As foreign powers attempt to invade the eastern coastal regions, divine intervention will alter the course of history. Enemy forces will face inexplicable setbacks—witnessing weapons failing mid-air and missile systems collapsing. This final battle will last only 5 days and 5 nights, leading to a decisive victory for Dharma.

Aftermath – The New World Order

Following these wars, the Bhavishya Malika describes a drastic transformation of human civilization. The world will rebuild itself, ushering in a spiritually enlightened era.

Key Predictions for the Future:

- A new societal system founded on truth, dharma, and harmony.
- A powerful spiritual awakening that reshapes human consciousness.
- The emergence of superhuman abilities, unlocking hidden potential.
- Earth's natural balance restored, bringing peace to the environment.
- Telepathic communication enabling mind-to-mind connection.
- Animals regaining their ability to speak, fostering deeper bonds with humans.

Bharata's Role in the New World:

- The *Bhavishya Malika* predicts that Bharata will rise as the spiritual leader of the world, setting an example of peace and divine governance.
- The world will witness the rebirth of Dharma, fulfilling the divine cycle of Yuga transformation.

Conclusion

The prophecies of the Bhavishya Malika offer a powerful vision of the future of humanity—a time of war, transformation, and ultimate rebirth. While the world may face destruction and chaos, those who walk the path of Dharma will witness the dawn of a golden age under the leadership of Kalki Avatar. This is not just a prophecy—it is a destined future, written in the cosmic order. Are we prepared for what is to come?

Disclaimer

This chapter is based on interpretations of ancient prophecies, scriptures, and spiritual traditions. The content should be understood in a symbolic and spiritual context, rather than as a literal prediction of future events. The views presented are based on historical texts and do not intend to promote fear, conflict, or hostility towards any individual, group, or nation. Readers are encouraged to approach this material with an open mind and use their personal judgment in interpreting these prophecies.

CHAPTER 19

THE FINAL LEELA OF LORD JAGANNATH

*M*ahaprabhu Jagannath is revered as the divine protector of Kali Yuga, and his abode, Puri Dham, is considered the holiest site of this age. As the ultimate Parabrahma—the soul of the cosmos—he has manifested in his original form to guide and protect his devotees from the malevolent grip of Kali. Yet, an astonishing truth remains: his divine Leela will conclude with the end of this Kali Yuga.

The Prophecy of Puri's Submergence

As foretold in ancient prophecies, the holy city of Puri will be swallowed by the sea. A catastrophic mega-tsunami is predicted to strike the eastern coast of India during the final battle of Kali Yuga. However, before this great deluge, a series of extraordinary events will unfold—events that will mark the last divine Leela of Mahaprabhu Jagannath.

Russia's Divine Mission and the Mysterious Train

As the great war rages and Bharata faces initial setbacks, Russia, recognizing the significance of Mahaprabhu Jagannath, will attempt to safeguard the Lord. Russian warriors will rush to Puri with the intent of carrying away the sacred idols of Lord Balabhadra, Maa Subhadra, and Lord Jagannath to protect them from falling into enemy hands. However, with war looming, their escape routes will be blocked.

In a desperate search for safe transport, the Russian warriors will arrive at Puri Railway Station. Awaiting them there will be an enigmatic steam engine—one that has long been whispered about in hushed tones. This engine, known as the *Pagala Engine* or the *Mad Engine*, is said to start and move on its own, requiring neither driver nor fuel. Though currently hidden in a secret location in Sealdah, West Bengal, this mystical train is still worshipped on specific dates by Hindu priests.

Using this divine locomotive, the Russian warriors will embark on their mission, carrying the sacred idols towards Paradip's seashore, where they hope to transport them to Russia via ships. But destiny has other plans.

The Devotees' Secret Intervention

As the train speeds through the night, it will mysteriously break down at Byree Station, an isolated and scarcely used railway stop. Hidden in the surrounding forests, devoted followers of Mahaprabhu Jagannath will await this moment. Under the cover of darkness, these devotees will stealthily confuse the Russian warriors and spirit away the idols to the sacred Jhadeshwar Kadhae, an ancient Shiva temple, where Lord Jagannath will be offered *Maha Prasad* for the final time in Kali Yuga.

The idols will then be transported to Chhatia Dham, the prophesied final resting place of Mahaprabhu Jagannath in this age. There, within hidden chambers of the temple, the sacred deities will be enshrined. When the mission is complete, the devotees will seek the blessings of Kalki Avatar and inform him of their success.

Kalki and Russia's Redemption

Upon learning that the idols are missing, the Russian warriors will follow their trail to Chhatia. There, they will encounter none other than Kalki Avatar himself. The divine incarnation will reveal to them the significance of this final Leela and convince them to join the forces of Dharma in the great war ahead.

Realizing their mistake, Russia will pledge allegiance to Kalki, aligning with the holy forces led by him and Lord Balaram. As their sacred duty, they will be entrusted with protecting Chhatia from enemy forces. With divine orders given, Kalki will march forward on his ultimate conquest—to annihilate *Adharma* and cleanse Bharata of its oppressors.

The Final Rath Yatra of Kali Yuga

After the great war is won, Kalki will return to Chhatia to seek the blessings of Mahaprabhu Jagannath. He will remind Russia of the boon granted by Lord Krishna in Dwapara Yuga—an opportunity to serve the Parambrahma in Kali Yuga.

In every *Rath Yatra*, the king must sweep the chariots before the grand procession begins. In the final *Rath Yatra* of this Yuga,

Russia will be granted the honor of becoming the ceremonial king, performing this sacred duty before Mahaprabhu Jagannath's last grand journey on earth.

Ancient texts reveal that Russia, known as the land of great sages (rishis) in Dwapara Yuga, had warriors who fought alongside the Pandavas in the Mahabharata. As a reward for their devotion and righteousness, Lord Krishna granted them this divine privilege—to serve him in his ultimate form as Mahaprabhu Jagannath in Kali Yuga.

The Eternal Slumber of Lord Jagannath

With his final Leela complete, Mahaprabhu Jagannath will return to his eternal abode in Puri Dham. He will enter his deep, divine slumber, awaiting the arrival of another Kali Yuga, when once again, he will manifest to guide and protect humanity.

Conclusion

And so, the divine play of Mahaprabhu Jagannath reaches its final act—the last sacred Leela of Kali Yuga. The echoes of his chariot wheels will fade, the temple bells will fall silent, and the ocean will claim the sacred land of Puri. But what remains is unshakable—faith that outlives time, devotion that no deluge can drown, and the eternal promise that no force in creation can break: *Dharma shall always prevail.*

Astonishing Facts & Hidden Mysteries

- **Byree Station's Mystery:** Byree Station in Odisha is one of the least crowded railway stations, receiving only a handful of passengers daily. Yet, Indian Railways has continued its maintenance, hinting at its hidden significance in the grand Leela.
- **Jhadeshwar Kadhae's Sacred Vow:** The priests of this temple never add salt in prasadam. They believe that only when Mahaprabhu Jagannath himself arrives to accept this *Prasadam* will they break this vow.
- **Chhatia Temple's Perpetual Construction:** The temple of Chhatia is under continuous expansion, operating 24/7, every single day of the year. When questioned about this, the temple authorities state that they are preparing for the grand final Leela of Mahaprabhu Jagannath.

CHAPTER 20

MEENA SHANI - THE FINAL CELESTIAL OMEN OF KALI YUGA

*M*ahaprabhu Jagannath's divine plan unfolds through celestial movements, and among them, the transit of Saturn into Pisces (Meena Shani) is one of the most significant omens of Kali Yuga's final phase. Ancient texts, including *Bhavishya Malika*, foretell that when Shani fully enters *Meena Rashi* on 29th March 2025, it will trigger a series of catastrophic events, leading to the great war, natural calamities, and the ultimate transition towards Satya Yuga.

The Prophecy of Meena Shani: What Lies Ahead?

According to the revered Saint Achyutananda Das, *Meena Shani's* impact will last 2.5 years, marking the final phase of Kali Yuga. This period is described as a time when:

- The **world will plunge into conflicts**—ongoing tensions will escalate, and new battles will emerge.
- **Massive natural disasters** will strike, with coastal cities facing devastating floods, storms, and earthquakes.

- Humanity will undergo a **spiritual transformation**, forced to turn towards *Dharma* for survival.

Mahapurusa Achyutananda Das describes an era of immense sufferings where food and water will become scarce. People will receive meals only once in fifteen days. The prophecy states:

Odia Verse:

"ଭକ୍ତ କୁଁ ନାନା କଷଣ ପଡିବ ଅର୍ଣ୍ଣ ଜଳ ନ ମିଳିବ ।
ପନ୍ଦର ଦିନରେ ଥରେ ଅର୍ଣ୍ଣ ଜଳ ସମୀର ଅଂକେ ଭୋଗିବ ।"

English Translation:

"Many Devotees will suffer greatly, struggling for food and water. They will receive a meal only once in fifteen days."

Scientific & Astrological Warning

Meena Shani coincides with a period of severe climate change, solar storms, and rising conflicts:

- **Solar Maximum & Geomagnetic Storms:** Scientists predict that by 2025, the Sun will enter its maximum solar phase, leading to unprecedented geomagnetic storms that could wipe out power grids and disrupt global communication.
- **Extreme Weather Events:** Record-breaking heatwaves, floods, and natural disasters will intensify beyond imagination.
- **Economic Collapse & New Diseases:** A global financial crisis and the emergence of unknown deadly diseases will parallel past pandemics.

The Beginning of the Final War

Saint Achyutananda Das explicitly states:

Odia Verse:

> "ମୀନ ଶନି ମେଳ ଗୋ ହୋଇବ ଯେତେ ବେଳେ ।
> ସେବେଳେ ସମର ହେବ ଭାରତ ମଣ୍ଡଳେ ।"

English Translation:

> "When Saturn will enter Pisces, war will break out in Bharata."

- This suggests that Bharat (India) will be at the center of the global war, aligning with modern geopolitical tensions.
- The war will be both spiritual and physical, marking the final phase as Kali Yuga's Mahabharata unfolds.

The Spiritual Awakening: A New Dawn After Destruction

Though this period will be one of suffering and chaos, Bhavishya Malika emphasizes that Meena Shani is not just about destruction—it is about transformation.

On 29 March 2025, Saturn entered Pisces marking the beginning of Satya Kali.

- The adverse conditions will push humanity toward the path of Dharma.

- A great spiritual awakening will arise, guiding people toward strength and victory.
- Bharat and its people will no longer submit—they will rise and establish Dharma's supremacy over the world.

The Road Ahead

The movement of Saturn into Pisces on 29 March 2025 is more than just an astrological shift—it is a cosmic signal of the final transformation. As humanity faces wars, disasters, and crises, only those who embrace Dharma and prepare for the coming struggles will survive and witness the dawn of Satya Yuga.

Thus, the prophecies of Meena Shani are not to instill fear but to guide humanity towards righteousness.

As the old world crumbles in fire and war, a new light will rise—not from kings or conquerors, but from those who walk the path of Dharma. Meena Shani is not the end—it is the moment where fate chooses who will perish in Kali Yuga and who will rise to witness the dawn of Satya Yuga.

CHAPTER 21

SATYA YUGA - DAWN OF A NEW AGE

The end of Kali Yuga is not merely an event; it is a cosmic transformation—a divine reset that will restore Dharma and purity to the world. According to ancient scriptures, including Bhavishya Malika, Satya Yuga is not a distant dream but an imminent reality. The process has already begun, and by 2029, Satya Yuga will unfold.

The Transition from Kali Yuga to Satya Yuga

The path from darkness to light is paved with trials, and the last days of Kali Yuga will be its most turbulent. Bhavishya Malika reveals that before Satya Yuga emerges, the world must endure its final purification:

- Wars will escalate, and civilizations will collapse under the weight of their own corruption.
- Natural calamities will purge the Earth, reshaping lands and washing away the remnants of Adharma.
- The final battle of Dharma vs. Adharma will witness the rise of Kalki Avatar, who will lead the righteous into the new era.

The New World of Satya Yuga

Unlike the corrupt and decaying world of Kali Yuga, Satya Yuga will be a golden age where everything functions in divine harmony. Scriptures describe this era as:

- **A world without deception**—where truth reigns supreme, and no one speaks falsehood.
- **A paradise of natural abundance**—where food grows effortlessly, and no one suffers from hunger or disease.
- **A realm of divine communication**—where humans will no longer need speech; and thoughts are transmitted through telepathy.

Mahapurusa Achyutananda Das foretold that in Satya Yuga:

Odia Verse:

"କୀଟ ପତଙ୍ଗ ମାନେ ଥିବେ ମାନବ ବଚନ କହିବେ ।
ଗୋମାତା କହିବେ ବଚନ ଏମନ୍ତ ବିଚାରିବେ ମନ ।"

English Translation:

"Insects and cows will converse like humans."

In this new era:

- **All living beings will gain spiritual consciousness**, breaking the barriers of language and species.
- **Humans will possess divine abilities**—teleportation, energy healing, and manifestation of their needs.

- **Life will be prolonged**, with an average human lifespan reaching 100,000 years, free from illness and suffering.

The Collapse of Materialism & the Rise of Divine Order

Satya Yuga will eradicate materialistic greed, making wealth irrelevant. The pursuit of money and power—hallmarks of Kali Yuga—will be replaced by universal abundance and equality.

- **A World Without Rich or Poor:** Wealth will lose its meaning as the Earth will naturally provide everything humans need. Fertile lands will flourish, rivers will flow with pure water, and nature will heal itself, offering abundance to all. The very concept of scarcity will vanish, replaced by a harmonious balance where every individual has access to life's essentials.
- **End of Greed, Jealousy, and Corruption:** With material wealth no longer being a measure of power, greed will dissolve, and the toxic desire to hoard possessions will fade. People will live in contentment, embracing a life of simplicity and inner peace. Deception, dishonesty, and manipulation will become relics of the past as humanity unites in trust and cooperation.
- **A Unified World Under Dharma:** The divisions of race, religion, and nationality will disappear as people awaken to their shared spiritual identity. The world will no longer be fragmented by ideologies or territorial disputes. Instead, all will follow the path of Dharma—a universal code of righteousness, compassion, and truth—creating a society where unity prevails and harmony flourishes.

Mahapurusa Achyutananda Das prophesied that in Satya Yuga:

Odia Verse:

"ଶସ୍ୟ ଧାନ ବହୁତ ସଂପଦ ଯେ ଲଭିବେ । ପ୍ରଭୁଙ୍କର ନାମକୁ ଯେ ଆନନ୍ଦେ ଗାଇବେ । ମହାସିଦ୍ଧ ନିଶବ୍ଦ ନିର୍ଘଣ୍ଟ ବ୍ରହ୍ମ ଏହି । ଶୁଣ ସାଧୁଜନମାନେ ସନ୍ତୋଷ ଯେ ହୋଇ ।"

English Translation:

"There will be no lack of wealth, no need for charity; only one feeling will exist—Devotion, Truth, and Love."

The Final Transformation: A Night That Will Change Everything

Odia Verse:

"ନିଶାରେ ଯେ ଜନମାନେ ଶୟନରେ ଥିବେ । ରାତ୍ର ଯେ ପାହିଲେ ସତ୍ୟବଚନ କହିବେ । ସତ୍ୟ କଳି ପ୍ରବେଶ ଜାଣିବୁ ସତ୍ୟ ସର୍ବ । ପ୍ରଭୁଙ୍କର ଆଜ୍ଞା ସେ ଯେ ମେଷଣ ହୋଇବ ।"

— ଅଚ୍ୟୁତାନନ୍ଦ ଦାସ

English Translation:

"In just one night, everything will change. Humans will begin to speak only truth, while all greed, envy, and pride will disappear."

— *Achyutananda Das*

Scriptures state that the shift from Kali Yuga to Satya Yuga will happen in an instant—within a single night. The entire world will undergo a radical transformation as Adharma dissolves into nothingness.

As the veil of illusion lifts, the true essence of life will be revealed. Humanity will awaken to its divine nature, leaving behind the suffering of the past Yuga.

Signs of Satya Yuga's Arrival

Bhavishya Malika outlines several unmistakable signs indicating Satya Yuga's imminent arrival:

- The return of Bhagwan Shri Ram to Ayodhya (fulfilled in 2024).
- The opening of all four doors of Jagannath Temple (fulfilled in 2024).
- A global awakening, where people across the world are turning towards Sanatana Dharma (Mahakumbh of 2025).

The Eternal Message of Satya Yuga

Satya Yuga is not merely a time period; it is a state of being—a world where:

- **Trust replaces fear**
- **Truth replaces deception**
- **Harmony replaces chaos**

The transition has already begun, and those who embrace Dharma and purity of heart will enter the new age.

As Bhavishya Malika proclaims:

Odia Verse:

"ଉଦୟ ଅସ୍ତ ଚୈତନ୍ୟ ରାତ୍ର ଦିବସ ନ ହୋଇବ ବାରଣ । ୪ ରଖୀ ୪ ଗୁଣ ଚେତି ଏହି ନାମ କର ଭଜନ ।"

English Translation:

"*Control your mind, purify your soul, and chant the name of Bhagwan. Those who do will witness the arrival of Satya Yuga.*"

Thus, Satya Yuga is not far—the question remains: Are you prepared for it?

CHAPTER 22

THE FINAL REVELATION - AWAKENING TO TRUTH

*T*he hour of reckoning has arrived. The world stands at the precipice of a great cosmic shift—an irreversible transition from the darkened age of Kali Yuga to the golden dawn of Satya Yuga. This is not mythology, nor is it mere speculation. The prophecies of Bhavishya Malika, concealed for centuries, have now been revealed so that mankind may awaken before it is too late.

This book is not just a collection of words; it is a divine beacon, a scripture that holds the final warning—the ultimate truth about our destiny. The time for hesitation has passed. Now is the moment to see, to understand, and to act.

The Great Transition

Kali Yuga—the age of deception, suffering, and moral decay—is crumbling before our very eyes. Wars rage across the lands, natural disasters intensify, and corruption infects the hearts of men. These are not coincidences. These are the preordained signs of the final purification.

Those who remain blind to the truth will be swept away in the storm. But those who stand firm in *Dharma* will endure. This is not just an external battle—it is the ultimate test of your soul's readiness. Will you be among those who awaken, or will you fall with the collapsing world order?

Karma & Dharma: Understanding the Law of Cosmic Justice

The greatest illusion of *Kali Yuga* is that actions have no consequences. This is the lie that fuels destruction.

Karma is real. Every action, every word, every thought shapes the destiny of your soul. The suffering of this world is not random—it is the direct result of humanity's abandonment of Dharma.

Dharma is not ritualistic practice. Dharma is the eternal cosmic law. It is truth, duty, righteousness. To uphold it is to align yourself with the divine. To abandon it is to invite chaos into your existence. The choice is yours, but know this—*Kali Yuga* will not spare those who choose ignorance.

The True Purpose of Human Birth

Why were you born in this age? Why were you given the gift of consciousness in a time of such great upheaval?

Bhavishya Malika reveals that human birth is not by chance. It is a sacred opportunity. You are here not to chase illusions, not to be enslaved by fleeting desires—but to transcend, to awaken, and to prepare for the new age.

You are not just flesh and bone. You are an eternal soul, bound only by the choices you make. Now, at the crossroads of time, you must choose your path.

The Hidden Knowledge Unveiled: The Role of This Book

For centuries, *Bhavishya Malika* was buried in obscurity, its truths withheld from the world. This book is not just a scholarly effort—it is a divine mission to restore what was lost.

It is important to understand that decoding the entire *Bhavishya Malika* manuscripts collection is not possible in a single lifetime, as the texts number in lakhs and are extraordinarily complex. However, if this edition is widely appreciated and readers express interest, I will wholeheartedly write a second edition, unveiling even more valuable insights.

This knowledge was not meant for profit or vanity. It was meant for the seekers, for warriors of truth, for those destined to carry *Dharma* into the next age. The hard work, the relentless research, the deep spiritual commitment behind this book was not for personal gain, but for humanity's awakening.

The question is—will you recognize its significance, or will you dismiss it as the world crumbles around you?

A Final Call to Action – With an Open Mind

This book is not written to create fear. It is not meant to divide. It is a message of preparation—a final call to those who are ready to hear.

If you doubt, question with sincerity. If you disagree, reflect before rejecting. But above all—do not ignore. The signs of Kali Yuga are before us. The prophecies are unfolding in real time. And soon, every soul will be confronted with the reality of this divine transition.

The end is not to be feared—it is to be embraced. Night does not last forever, and this Darkness is but a prelude to dawn. And those who walk the path of truth will rise with this dawn. The final question remains: Are you prepared for it?

A MESSAGE FROM THE HEART

*A*s you turn the final page of this book, I am filled with immense gratitude. This journey—decoding the sacred prophecies of the Bhavishya Malika—was not just a pursuit of knowledge, but a mission of the soul.

To you, the seeker who walked this path with me, I offer my heartfelt thanks. Every word you have read, every thought you have reflected upon, and every moment you devoted to understanding these ancient revelations is a testament to your courage — the courage to seek truth in a world clouded by deception.

The wisdom of the Bhavishya Malika is not easily unveiled. Its secrets are vast, its messages deeply coded, and its meanings layered with spiritual depth. I have shared what I could in this humble effort, yet I know there is still so much more waiting to be revealed. If this book has touched your heart, sparked your curiosity, or awakened something deeper within you, I promise to continue this sacred mission. With your curiosity as my inspiration, I hope to unveil more truths from these ancient manuscripts in the future.

But for now, I ask you to carry forward what you have learned. Let the message of *Dharma* guide your thoughts, actions, and choices. Be the light that others seek in this dark hour of *Kali Yuga*. The dawn of truth is near — and your role in this awakening is greater than you may realize.

May the blessings of Mahaprabhu Jagannath and the divine guidance of Panchasakha illuminate your path.

Jay Jagannath!

With deepest gratitude and unwavering hope,
Sachin Mohapatra, Author

Connect with me for more meaningful insights:

YouTube: https://www.youtube.com/@ViralOdisha

Instagram: https://www.instagram.com/viralodishahindi

Facebook: https://www.facebook.com/viralodishahindi

Twitter/X: https://twitter.com/viral_odisha

Email: viralodisha1@gmail.com

Your purchase supports the welfare of stray animals.

If you loved the book, I'd be grateful if you could leave an honest review —

Your words will help spread this knowledge far and wide.

"This book is a part of Project K."

www.ingramcontent.com/pod-product-compliance
Lightning Source LLC
LaVergne TN
LVHW061551070526
838199LV00077B/7001